Black Folks' Guide to
Making Big Money in America

Black Folks' Guide to Making Big Money in America

by

George Trower-Subira
B.A., M.Ed., Ed.S.

Published by
Very Serious Business Enterprises
P.O. Box 356
Newark, New Jersey 07101
UNIVERSAL BOOKS
51 COURT STREET
WHITE PLAINS, NEW YORK 10601
(914) 681-0484

First Printing, July 1980
Second Printing, December 1980
Third Printing, June 1981
Fourth Printing, October 1981
Fifth Printing, July 1982
Sixth Printing, September 1982
Seventh Printing, November 1982
Eighth Printing, November 1983
Ninth Printing, October 1983
Tenth Printing, October 1985
Eleventh Printing, November 1985
Twelfth Printing, March 1987
Thirteenth Printing, April 1988
Fourteen Printing, September 1989
Fifteenth Printing, June 1991

FIRST EDITION

ISBN 0-960-53040-1

This book is dedicated to goo gobs of people; all have been important in my development thus far.

To the folks, George Sr. and Roxanna, who planted enough of the right seeds that I never had anything to really worry about.

To Mfuasi for being the strongest encouragement for this book.

To Pansy, my love, for making it even more obvious why this book had to be written.

To Jabali who always helped keep my head together.

To Mtume, Marion, Bob Pickett, and Doctors Montique and G. Jackson for being such incredible examples of strength and determination.

To Dr. Ron Karenga, my greatest teacher—I owe you in spite of yourself.

This book is dedicated to the master promoters of the Black world—Muhammad Ali, James Brown, Berry Gordy, Reverend Ike, Reggie Jackson, Don King, George "Dr. Funkenstein" Clinton, Bootsy "Casper" Collins and Barbara Gardner Proctor.

This book is dedicated to the future in the persons of Ibn, Dadisi and Tamani.

And a special thanks to Wendy Gibson, Janice Carter, Diane Hill, Jinni Bailey, Elaine Johnson and Pansy for fighting through my chicken scratch and typing out a presentable manuscript.

Thanks to Mrs. Margot Banks for adding some of the King's English to my Black English. Final editing by Maisha Alake Zulu.

And a very special thanks to James Lucas—Brother you were right on time!

Contents

Introduction

Hello, my name is George Trower Subira and what you have in your hands right now is my book, *Black Folks Guide to Making Big Money in America.* I'd like to explain a few things to you about this book, such as why it was written, how it is written and how to use the book.

This guide was written to answer a need that has been quite obvious now for hundreds of years. Specifically, the problem is how do you teach the former slaves to obtain their share of the wealth that they largely created in this country. I believe that it is a shame that you, the Black public, have had to wait so long for a book like this to be available to you.

Africans arrived in America officially in 1619 (many say sooner), and from that year to this one we have had severe economic problems. Now in three hundred and sixty years you would think that someone, Black or White, would have determined that this problem of Black poverty was serious enough to merit at least one book discussing the solutions to the problems. Wouldn't you? I assumed that this book had been done years ago. But when I asked bookstore owners and librarians for books on learning how to make money from Black folks' perspective, they just sort of looked at me. You could just about hear what they were thinking (Is this nigga crazy?).

I want you to understand that there are many books on the market discussing Black capitalism, Black business, the economics of the ghetto, etc. But there has been no book, up to this point, ever written for Mr. Average Black Man, or Woman, to read, study, and use to build a comfortable, safe, secure life for himself and his family. And that, my friend, is exactly why this book was written.

There were other reasons besides extreme need which caused me to write this book. The most important (as you may have guessed) was money. I truly believe that this investment will bear substantial fruit or else it would not have been written. Competition was another factor. I want many more writers, business persons and scholars to begin writing on this theme. It doesn't matter to me whether they mention me, blast my ideas or support them, as long as you, the public, have more relevant information to select from than you have had in the last three hundred and sixty years.

Another factor motivating me to write this book was the prospect of

1

meeting new friends and/or business partners. I love to work with serious people on projects that create social development, excitement and profit. I'm always game for development and profit.

HOW TO BEST USE THIS BOOK

The best way to use this book is to read it! That might sound stupid but ask yourself how many books do you own that you have never read? This book contains both facts and philosophy. I have found that a person needs both information (facts) and the proper attitude (or philosophy) in order to be successful in any venture. If I had written a plain step-by-step plan of how to make money with no discussion of Black folks and White folks attitudes, I don't think you would have been too convinced to take the program very seriously. On the other hand, if I would have rapped for days on a philosophy of money without showing a concrete program, you would have probably accused me of fraud. So I have combined both philosophic and practical statements to come up with this program designed to take the serious Black person from poverty to wealth.

At the risk of sounding boastful, I will recommend that you not try to fully comprehend everything in this book on the very first reading. This book is a guide—not a novel. You do not read this book, put it down and go on about your business as usual. It was not designed that way. What you should do is read it, think about it and then go out and attempt to do something (anything) to improve your financial situation. Later, you come back and reread a point, section or the entire book that may now have taken on a different meaning. Making big bucks, especially if you are Black, is a long and often difficult process. The purpose here is to show you some correct methods of looking at and doing things which should shorten the road to wealth considerably.

You could also gain a great deal of additional insight by reading this book in a study group or discussing it with friends or family. I have often found that among Black folks we often disagree on ideas because we refuse to give our buddy credit for seeing a problem from a better perspective or giving it a better analysis than ourselves. Rather than agree to what seems like the more logical or reasonable answer, we get upset and yell something like, "Hey, well that's just your opinion, man!" We then go our separate ways knowing that the other person was right but somehow believing that we won something simply by being stubborn and refusing to give in on the point. This problem has certainly caused a lack of collective effort in many money making situations. If you used a common book (this one), you wouldn't feel like you had to "win" or "lose" with any person; you could merely discuss the book. Law students, medical students and other graduate students use study groups to get through school. Why can't you form a study group to learn how to actually make some money. If enough of your friends (potential partners) can agree on enough ideas, you may decide to actually start a business project. I mean if you're serious!

In any event this book is only intended to be the beginning of your financial education. It will point you to other valuable sources of information. You the reader, however, must have the curiosity and the energy to hunt down the right people, books and information that you need to do your thing. Without learning enough to raise the right questions you will not get the right answers. Without the right answers a lot of time, work and money may be wasted.

As Brother George Clinton (Dr. Funkenstein) of Parliament Funkadelic has always said, "Free your mind and your ass will follow. Think! It ain't illegal yet."

Later,

Subira

Coming to Grips
with Your Financial Ignorance

When I was a college instructor teaching mostly Black youth, I found that one of the biggest barriers to students learning had nothing to do with their not coming to class, missing reading assignments or poor study habits. One of the biggest barriers was the fact that students already felt they knew the subject matter being taught. Others knew they didn't know very much but felt they knew enough to satisfy their curiosity and "get over" which was, after all, all they were interested in. It is very, very difficult to pass on information to anybody if they feel that they already know enough for their satisfaction. Another complicating factor is that there are certain topics that people don't like to admit they're ignorant of. For instance, no lady will really advertise the fact that she can't cook. No man would like to be caught scratching his head wondering how to change a flat tire because almost all men and all women expect all men to know how to change a flat tire. There are other subjects, like sex for example, where you never ask a question which might reveal ignorance.

Money, the topic of this book, is one of these forbidden topics that people don't like to talk too much about. About the most you can expect people to do is complain about money or the lack of it.

It is my duty, I believe, to spend some time helping you to come to grips with your financial ignorance if I'm to do my primary job which is to teach you a few tricks on how to improve your finances, lifestyle and bank account. It's sort of like a doctor having to convince a patient that they're seriously sick so that they will take their medicine or a lawyer convincing a defendant of the seriousness of the charges against him so that he will tell the truth. Basically, there are four things which I think make up the greatest part of our financial ignorance:

1. We really don't know what wealth is and how many ways it can be measured.
2. We poor folks have very little knowledge of what the rich folks do to get their money and hold on to it.
3. We really do not understand how our own habits keep us in the poor house and keep us from seeing and doing what the rich do.

4

4. We have very little understanding of the extremely strong influence that our attitudes about ourselves, money, work and life in general affect our ability to gain and build wealth.

The purpose of the next three chapters is to give a broader understanding of the four topics listed above. I believe it is only by admitting to yourself the shortcomings of your understanding of wealth and poverty that you can open your mind to new information. The new information will hopefully get you excited about the many possibilities and you will *go out into the world and do it.*

What Is Wealth?

How can ambitious, bright, energetic and talented folks build wealth and a comfortable lifestyle for their family if they don't know what wealth is? Is wealth defined by how much money a person makes in a year? Is wealth simply the fact that a person has a very attractive home, car and wardrobe and otherwise *appears* to be doing ok? Is wealth having a fat bank account? Do wealthy people put their money in banks? These are just a few questions that you will have to have answers for in order for you to feel comfortable with your own definition of wealth. You have to stretch your imagination to better understand the meaning of wealth, and if you can do that, you are at least one step closer to the goal.

Let's examine a number of things that all relate to this concept or idea of wealth.

1. *WEALTH IS RELATED TO THE* TOTAL *NET CASH COMING IN PER WEEK, MONTH OR YEAR.*

Most of us easily understand the idea of making a certain number of dollars per week or per year. In higher circles, this is known as "cash flow," meaning that there is a regular flow of cash each pay period. For most of us the source of this cash flow is our job, business or profession. Having a consistently "high" weekly or yearly inflow of cash is what most people mean by wealthy.

This consistent flow of cash enables most of us to deal with the consistent flow of bills and expenses that we generate in our daily lives. If we are fortunate enough to be able to pay all of our "flowing bills" with our "flowing cash"—we are surviving. If there is a good deal of surplus cash remaining after we pay all our bills (called disposable income), then we could be considered "wealthy," at least by some of those who do not have this surplus cash.

The key word in the statement above, however, is the word *total*. Wealthy people, you see, almost always have more than one form of income. That other income could come from investments in stocks, real estate, or any of a thousand other sources. The key point, however, remains that wealth is related to having more than one source of income. We will look into this point later on in the book.

2. *WEALTH IS RELATED TO IMMEDIATE ACCESS TO CASH.*

We all work for money, right? When is the best time to have money? When you really need it . . . right? If that set of facts is so clear, so obvious and so accepted, then why don't people have money when they need it? What is the point of working 50 or 49 weeks out of every year if you cannot respond with needed cash in emergency situations (within twenty-four hours)?

Wealth is the ability to respond to emergencies and opportunities. Emergencies and opportunities usually have one thing in common— they require you to respond fast with cash or you'll lose out, period.

I don't care how much money your doctor, lawyer or dentist makes, nor where he lives, how his home is furnished nor what kind of car he/she drives. If they cannot raise the quick money needed to take care of life's most critical moments, they are not wealthy. I'm sure most of us would rather have money when we really need it than spend it lavishly when we're not in financial stress. Wealthy people do both.

3. *WEALTH IS RELATED TO ONE'S TOTAL BORROWING CAPACITY.*

You may have noticed by now that you have to be rich to borrow any money these days. The bank wants to know if we already have (in valuables or assets) the amount of money that we're seeking to borrow. We ask to borrow ten thousand dollars and the banker responds by saying, "Ok, what have you got that's worth ten thousand dollars?" We stare at him for a second and begin to boil, then slowly stand up and walk away.

Wealth is the ability to have quick access (say three to five days or so) to a large sum of money. Where do the wealthy store this money? That is a good question because most people think the wealthy store their money in savings accounts. That is usually not the case. The wealthy's money is stored in the value of their home, insurance policies, some savings accounts, stocks and bonds, and other types of investment funds, business accounts, outstanding business debts, gold, silver and jewelry, and a whole host of other appreciating (gaining in value) assets (possessions). Some folks have more money hanging on their wall (valuable art work) in their living room than we will make in the next ten years. In any event there are ways to "hock" or borrow money on any kind of valuable item. You may be wondering about now, "Why is this guy continuing to harp on borrowing money? Wealthy people don't need to borrow money because they already got it . . . right? Wrong. We make money in little bitty pieces week to week, and we do it by working. Wealthy people make money in chunks all at once, and they do it by borrowing. Let's see:

As I am writing this book, gold is going absolutely crazy, beserk. Around Thanksgiving 1979, gold was worth may be $425 an ounce, and by the week after New Year's it was about $610 an ounce. Now let's say I'm wealthy and have a good income and somebody calls me on November 15th and says, "Hey Subira, go buy some gold; it's going to go through the roof in a couple of months."

Now you can't buy gold like you do penny candy. You can't go to a precious metal broker and say, "One ounce of gold please." you've got to buy a block of gold to make it worth anybody's effort. But first I go to the bank and borrow some money. The banker says, "I see here you make 100K* per year, your house is worth 150K but you only owe 46K on it. How much would you like to borrow?" I say, "Eighty thousand." "Fine, Mr. Subira, I'll draw the papers up this afternoon and you can come in tomorrow to pick up your check." I take the check to the gold dealer and say, "I want 80K in gold." "Yes sir," the dealer says, "here is your certificate certifying your purchase of 188 ounces of gold." (You see, 188 ounces at $425 per ounce comes to 80K.)

Now between Thanksgiving and New Year's, I do what everybody else does that time of year. I watch football, drink egg nog, buy holiday presents and kiss women under the mistletoe (and other nice places).

After New Year's Day is over and gone, I look in the paper and see that in those forty-five days or so, my 188 ounces of gold is now worth over one hundred and fourteen thousand dollars. That, my friend is thirty-four thousand dollars ($34,000) in gross profit in a month and a half time. Now what work did I do? What money did I spend? Now do you see why the wealthy borrow big sums of money? You have got to be *worth it* to *borrow it*. You've got to invest it to make more, and it all takes very little energy either physically or mentally. How much did you make between Thanksgiving and New Year's?

4. *WEALTH IS TOTAL NET WORTH.*

The closest measure that anyone can use to determine how wealthy they are is to figure out their total net worth. Unfortunately, in the Black community that is almost a foreign concept. What do

*NOTE: K will be used to represent $1,000. Thus, 46K = $46,000 . . . ok?

you mean total net worth? Total net worth means determining the dollar value of everything you own and totaling the whole sum up and then subtracting from this sum all the debts that you owe. The final number that is left is your net worth. It is important to understand that it is not always easy to put a dollar value on the things you own. Sometimes people use the figure that they paid for something as the dollar value, and that is most often not the case.

For example: In January you buy a new living room set for $1,000. You put down $200 cash and make payments of $40 a month on the $800 balance. You have three kids who love to eat in the living room and an uncle who visits once a month and always drops his cigar ashes because he talks so much. You had two parties during the year and your baby cousin wet on the sofa when he slept over one weekend. In December you're trying to figure out your net worth and you come to the furniture. What is it worth? You've paid $440 in payments, so you add that to the $200 downpayment and that comes to a $640 investment so far. But 50% of the first year's payments went to interest charges so your bill is still $600. What is the net worth of your furniture now eleven months old with cigarette burns, wear and tear and a faint urine odor? Well, first you have to figure out what you could sell this furniture for if you had to, or what would a furniture store give you on a trade-in. Guess! Five hundred dollars, maybe? Suppose you could get $500 for your used furniture; you then mark $500 down in the *asset* column. Now you owe $600 still, so you subtract $600 from $500 and you get minus one hundred dollars (−$100). That means your furniture is not really considered an asset in terms of your financial worth at that point.

Poor folks often have a minus net worth which means what they owe is greater than the value (the sale value) of what they have. A typical net worth statement may look something like this:

Assets Value		Debts	
House	32K	House Mortgage	27K
Car	4K	Car	2K
Savings	2K	Charge Cards	1.5K
Cash Value of Insurance Policy	.5K	Dept. Store Bills	1K
House Furnishings & Appliances	1K	Doctor Bill	.2K
Clothes	.2K	School Loan	3K
Stereo and TVs	.8K	Personal Bank Loan	1K
Jewelry	.2K		
	$40,700		$35,700

$40,700
−35,700

$ 5,000 NET WORTH

In the above illustration, you have a net worth of about five thousand dollars. If you were to die and all your bills were paid from the assets you left behind, you might (and I mean might) have a thousand dollars left over. Why? Because there are all kinds of hidden costs, especially legal fees and taxes, when a person dies. Also, the family will not sell all the assets. Someone will take the t.v., somebody else will get the refrigerator and sofa and so on.

When anybody lends money, they want to "see your statement;" that means your personal balance sheet, your net worth. Wealthy folks have all kinds of crazy things in their statements, crazy that is, to the Black community who has never learned to understand this kind of stuff.

Let's look at just a few normal kinds of assets and then look at some unusual ones:

"Normal" Wealth Assets of Sandra Miller		*Debts*
Home	100K	50K
Summer Home	50K	25K
Stocks, Bonds	25K	0
Antiques and Art Work	15K	0
Coin Collection	7K	0
Stamp collection	25K	0
Boat & Scuba Gear	15K	7K
Family Business & Real Estate	100K	22K
	337K —	104K = 233K

All of the above assets are pretty straight forward. The assets show that this person has two homes with a total value of 150K but with two mortgages totaling 75K. Thus, her equity (net worth in dollars) in her two homes is 75K.

Sandra is a collector. She collects rare stamps and rare coins. Not only does she find this fascinating and a way to make good friends but it is also very profitable. Sandra's two collections are worth 32K and will be likely to rise in value each and every year. The boat and scuba gear are down by the summer home and have maintained their value because new boats and gear keep going up in price. The family business is a storefront shoe shop and includes not only all the shoe inventory in the store but the whole building which includes a rented store on the corner and five apartments on the second floor. A mortgage of 22K is still to be paid off. This is a typical upper middle class White family asset statement.

"Unusual" Assets   *Debts*

19 years remaining on the lease at 100 Broadway	75K	0
15 Billboards on Route 40	50K	0
Liquor License at Seashore	35K	0
Publishing Rights to 1977 Novel	100K	0
Copyright to *I Love Moscow in* *the Springtime*	100K	0

The items above are also assets but are rather different than the "normal" ones explained above. Let me explain the rather weird things that wealthy folks leave behind for their kids to keep or sell.

a) A lease is a signed agreement to rent a space for a certain period of time at a specified sum of money. In this case our wealthy person got a twenty-five year lease and died after the first six years. The rental agreement gave our dead friend here the right to transfer all his rights at anytime before the twenty-five years are up. The rents have more than doubled since Mr. X here took his lease out six years before. People are ringing the phone off the hook to see if they can take over his building space with that lease. The family finally agrees to sell the lease (in other words, sell the right to pay cheap rent for the next 19 years) to a law firm that was expanding. The law firm figures that over twenty years they would save $250,000 in rent costs if they were able to get Mr. X's lease. The family sells the lease for $75,000. The terms are $50,000 down and the rest over a year's time.

The law firm is happy because they got a good location for a cheap rent for the next 19 years saving them over $175,000. The family got $50,000 in cash and $500 per week for the next year.

b) Fred rented his billboard spaces to companies along Route 40 and made about $15,000 per year doing it. When he died he left the billboards to his family. They can simply handle the old accounts or sell to John. John pushes hard and offers $50,000. The family takes the 50K. John is happy because he's getting a 30% return on his money every year and he doesn't have to do any work because the companies put up their own signs.

c) Bill lives in a seashore town where he use to own a bar. He sold the bar to a health food store and they made it a health bar. Bill kept his liquor license and the town stopped issuing new licenses. There are only a limited number of licenses available. Bill is the only owner of a liquor license that doesn't own a bar. A couple of luxury condominiums are built near the beach and the developer wants to put a restaurant in the complex. He knows he needs to serve liquor if he's going to get any decent business. Bill dies. Bill's family wants to move to California. They sell the license that they have no use for $35,000. The condo developer is happy because he managed to get a license even though the town wasn't issuing any more.

d) Jake from Seattle wrote a novel about seal hunting and it bombed. Nobody bought the book because seal hunting wasn't an issue when the book first came out. Jake was very disappointed. He worked for two years writing this book and got no money; nothing in return. All of a sudden seal hunting becomes a national issue and his book sales have hit the roof. Jake dies in an helocopter crash while filming a seal hunt. A television producer calls up the mourning family and says he wants to do a movie from Jake's book to dramatize the issue of seal hunting and also as a memorial to Jake. The family agrees. Their attorney tells the producer the rights to the book will cost them 100 thousand. The television station says ok. The program makes money, the family makes money and the lawyer makes money. The television program does an excellent job getting across the ideas Jake was trying to express. The t.v. program causes book sales to double and thus brings the fatherless family that much more income.

e) Eric Mann is an elderly man who lives in Detroit. Mr. Mann was a song writer in his day but he only had one hit record, "I love Moscow in the Springtime." His other efforts brought him much more personal satisfaction than money. Today, "I Love Moscow in the Springtime" is still being played on your middle of the road radio stations and in Europe even though the record is twenty years old. A few thousand copies of the record are sold every year. All toll, "I Love Moscow in the Springtime" still brings Mr. Mann about 15K per year in various royalties fees. Mr. Mann would really like to leave Detroit and move to California to be nearer his son and grandchildren. They live in a condominium which Mr. Mann cannot afford on his present income. One day our composer decided to sell all rights to his song and publishes this in a popular music composer's journal. A West German hot shot who's hit it big decides that he'll buy the rights from Mr. Mann for 100K. Mr. Mann accepts and is able to go to California and buys his condominium for cash. He's very happy to be with his grandchildren. Mr. Barz, the West German whiz kid, does a disco version of "I Love Moscow in the Springtime" with his hit band. The record soars to the top of the charts, and Mr. Barz makes a mint of money in royalties and concert performances. But, the revival of the song causes the older version of the record to rise in sales greatly also. Five years later, Mr. Barz is still collecting a great deal of money off sales of the older version after his disco hit is off the scene.

All of the little stories explained above were written with one thing in mind and that was to expand your idea of what an asset is. Anything that can be sold to another because it has an obvious, or sometimes not so obvious, value is an asset. These assets can be merely the right to collect money from something that is involved in the process of doing business. As we have seen, even a license or lease, if it is important enough to the type of business you are doing, can be considered an asset and therefore has a monetary value. If they have a monetary value then they can also be used as collateral to borrow money.

5. WEALTH IS RELATED TO ONE'S HOME ENVIRONMENT.

It's one thing for a person to be powerless to control the politics or economics of his or her neighborhood. But it is something different all together to be powerless in your own home. Poor people are told everyday what they can and cannot do in their own homes. They are told they can't have pets, loud music, long parties, musical instruments or dish washers. They are told how many children they can have sleeping in each room and are told they cannot keep relatives and friends housed for more than a few days. In short, poor folks are told exactly how to live within the space that they occupy and pay for.

Wealthy people, on the other hand, enjoy a freedom and control over their living space. They have loud music, pets, musical instruments and any other thing which they desire because they usually own their space and there is ample room for them to do their thing and not bother their neighbors. This is one of the advantages of having a private home.

I have noticed that poor folks seek relief, excitement, pleasure and comfort *out* of their house while the wealthy enjoy these things *in* their house. For the wealthy, a home is a major source of pride and they enjoy entertaining friends and family there. For the poor, home is not likely to be the place where you would invite new friends, and you clearly seek not to be personally judged on the basis of the condition of your home.

In short, there are tremendous emotional and psychological differences that exist between the contentment that wealthy persons enjoy in their homes and the frustration that poor folk experience in theirs. As if all these differences were not enough, it just so happens that there is a financial impact also. Pleasant, spacious homes will always go up in value. Sometimes the increase in value can be as much as 100K a year or more in some very prestigious neighborhoods. This is another example of how the rich get richer and do so with such enjoyment and contentment year after year.

6. *WEALTH IS RELATED TO LIFESTYLE.*

It is always important to keep in mind that the major purpose of money is to provide a lifestyle that is pleasurable, exciting and totally satisfying to our principles. It does no purpose to simply grow in net worth, monthly income and borrowing capacity if the things that make life worth living are not yours to enjoy. For this reason one should be careful not to always associate how much a person makes a year as being the reliable measure of their wealth. Let us look at a couple of examples:

a) Sam is a legal corporate executive with a New York firm that deals in lumber. His salary is 60K per year. His job requires him to spend most of his time in the New York office reading over and preparing contracts and reports for his company. He does not get out to see the company operations very often because most of their clients are in the states of Washington, Oregon and Montana. Sam has good health and life insurance benefits from his job and gets three weeks of paid vacation a year. Sam is very happy in his job because he really loves legal work, and he is the highest paid person in his company other than the president and the executive vice president. Somehow, though, Sam feels he is missing something out of life.

b) Stan is an independentfilm producer, and his company had tripled its gross revenue in the last year. Stan decided for tax purposes to cut down his salary and restructure the company finances because he could see that the next three years were going to be biggies and he hated paying all that money to Uncle Sam.

Stan bought a company car (Mercedes Benz) and gave himself an expense account. Most lunches are shared with actors or other film people, as are many dinners, so Stan's company pays for the majority of his meals (Stan skips breakfast). There are six film festivals which Stan is scheduled to attend this year. One festival is in Paris, another in Honolulu, and the rest in Grenada, Rio De-Janerio, Rome and Tokyo. Naturally, this is company business so the business will pay for all expenses.

As the business increased there was more presure on Stan, so the company paid for Stan's membership at a local health spa and gave him a complete physical exam twice a year.

One of Stan's accounts was a business firm that wanted some training films produced. Stan notices that some of the information the company wanted explained on film was also the same information that he felt he needed to understand to better run his own company. Thus, our man with the camera became a student for three weeks in the fall taking three comprehensive courses at a special seminar at Harvard. The cost for the course, room and board, books and study aids came to three thousand dollars. Naturally, the company paid for this doubly important educational program.

Finally, it became obvious that the long attempts by Stan to break into a piece of the Hollywood scene had finally paid off. The only problem was that the constant travel from New York to Los Angeles was costing a fortune. The company made the decision to set up a branch office in Hollywood, so Stan now occupies a condominium out there that doubles as an office and living quarters. The toll-free telephone system allows him to keep in contact with his New York secretary and a few friends. Naturally, the company pays.

Stan, like Sam, gets 60K a year in salary. He saves at least half of it and decided he didn't need a vacation this year.

It should be pretty obvious that although Sam and Stan make the same salary, they live totally different lifestyles. Sam would not only have to make at least twice the salary to live like Stan, but he couldn't squeeze it into his three free weeks anyway.

7. WEALTH IS RELATED TO LEISURE TIME.

Most of us work a job. The job, regardless of what kind it is, usually demands that we give forty-nine or fifty weeks out of our fifty-two week year. Think about that! We spend better than 96% of our time working to further advance the ambitions and goals of someone else's company, name, image and/or profits. In exchange, we get a salary that never quite seems to pay for our needs. The only free time that we really have are weekends where household duties and routines eat up more precious time; holidays where rush hour traffic problems create a drag; and finally, our vacation. In two weeks we try to reward ourselves and our families for the work, struggle and sacrifice that we've done for the entire year.

Even enterprising businesspeople can find themselves chained to the work place not only fifty weeks or more but the holidays as well, if holidays figure into their normal business schedule.

It is no wonder that you often hear that old saying, "What's the use of making good money if you don't have time to enjoy it." There is a lot of truth to this statement. The key phrase is "good money." You will never be able to have leisure time (I call it buying your

time back) as long as you merely make "good money." You have
to actually be wealthy to be able to pass up opportunities to earn
income so that you can do what you want to do.

Look at it this way: Most of us earn between 25 to 100 dollars
a day. "Good money" to most people would be from 100 to 200
dollars a day. Very few of us can *afford* (the *key* word) to give
up a week's time ($125-$1,000 in pay) simply to do something
that we enjoy. Those of us who think we could afford it couldn't
really afford it. Why? Because we might be able to maintain our
lifestyle with the loss of a week's pay, but our supervisor or "boss"
would not let us continue our employment if we tried to take off
more than once. Could you afford the loss of your job?

The borderline businessman is in the same position as the worker
or worse. He or she would not only lose the income from a week's
operation if they closed, but the possible loss in patronage or reputation may vibrate through the company for months.

Who then can afford the luxury of controlling their own time?
The wealthy! The wealthy person's assets, income and lifestyle is
set up in such a way that one week, one month or perhaps a year of
"free" time will not greatly affect their way of living. The reasons
are due not just to the fact that they are wealthy but due to the
characteristics (explained in a later chapter) fortune builders use
to gain wealth in the first place.

Remember this: In this life you will run out of time before you
run out of money. We know this because almost all of us leave some
kind of money or valuables behind after we die. If this is so, then
isn't time more valuable than money? If time is more valuable than
money, why should we use the most important thing (time) to make
the less important thing (money)? If time is more important than
money, can you be wealthy with just money?

8. *WEALTH IS RELATED TO DEFENSE.*

I was told by a wise man that all of life could be put in essentially
two categories: development or defense. In this life you are either
developing something or defending what you have already developed.
One must develop wealth in order to keep it. In this country Black
folks have made great fortunes, but it was the area of defense where
circumstances or White folks took it away.

Wealthy people usually have friends or allies in high places.
Sometimes the wealthy intermingle with the powerful for special
favors or prestige. But whatever the reason, defense is certainly high

on the list of priorities. Let's look at a few failures of Black folks to defend their wealth.

a) Land was the greatest source of wealth for Black folks in this country. We had 15 million acres in 1920 or so. Now in 1980 we own maybe 6 million and are losing about 10,000 acres a week due to the lack of our ability as a people to defend ourselves against its loss.

b) Muhammad Ali was a very wealthy man in the 1960's. When certain interests in this country decided to move against Ali and take away the source of his wealth, he was not in a position to immediately defend against it. He lost the two most important things going for him—time and money—during that period.

c) Another boxer-athlete, Joe Louis, suffered from a poor defense. Louis made a lot of money in the boxing ring, but a series of events including a bout with the Federal Income Tax Service knocked him for a loss.

d) Paul Robeson was perhaps the greatest Black superman that was ever born among Africa's offspring in the Western world. The man could do everything, and he was wealthy at one time. But when this nation moved to silence Paul Robeson, not only could he not defend his wealth and means of earning a living but his very name disappeared from American history and society, and he was treated as if he didn't even really exist.

Long after Black folks as individuals and as a people become wealthy (we are already among the wealthiest on the planet earth), the challenge of defense will still be there staring us in the face. Defense is closely allied to political and military power. It is difficult for everyone to ever feel that they have done enough to feel secure in their defense. The United States, the wealthiest nation, spends more on defense than anything else, as do the Russians and Chinese. And sometimes even all the money in the world can't buy a good defense. The former Shah of Iran had more money than any 100 wealthy people could want and his defense was still shaky.

9. WEALTH IS RELATED TO REPUTATION AND RESPECT.

In almost every country in the world (and yes the nations of Africa also), there is an almost automatic respect given to the wealthy. I believe many people go after wealth when all they ever really wanted was the popularity and/or respect that comes with it.

I have seen in the last 15 years in the Black community that many persons have been verbally attacked, ridiculed and criticized.

Sammy Davis Jr., Sidney Poitier, Muhammad Ali, John Johnson (Ebony Magazine), Diana Ross, Joe Frazier, Wilt Chamberlain and Diahann Carroll, among others, all had to withstand a lot of verbal abuse from the Black community at one time or another. Usually this negative backlash resulted from having too much money or too close an association with White folks or both.

But, when our controversial figures actually entered a room, walked on a stage or made some type of public appearance, all the bad talk faded away, and there was always applause, pride, envy and respect. Always. Why? I really can't tell for sure. Maybe each star has a certain thing that acts as a turn on. But, I know—I'm absolutely sure—that their wealth has a lot to do with it. I've sat back and watched the loudmouths do a complete reversal when actually confronted by the so-called "jive turkey." Instead of calling names, they look at the long flashy limosine, the militant security guards, the fine clothes, gleaming jewelry and the busy photographers, and all of a sudden our "jive turkey" becomes the "star" again. Some of these so-called critics are the first to ask for autographs.

I've heard it said that money can't buy you respect. Don't you believe it!

10. WEALTH IS RELATED TO INDEPENDENCE.

Independence is a vague term because no one is ever actually totally independent of other people. We all need people to develop our wealth and defend our interests in dangerous or threatening situations.

We are all dependent on having good relationships with different types and levels of persons to make our own life pleasant. If this is the case, and I believe it is, what then is independence? Independence to me is a lack of extreme dependence on any one job, person, organization, institution, idea, skill, location or other variable. Wealth is related to the idea that if one opportunity doesn't succeed then another just as good (maybe better) will. Independence says that my lifestyle, assets, and income are not so totally connected to any one thing that the destruction of that one thing is the same as the destruction of me. Independence, like defense, can be harder to gain than wealth itself. Independence is a form of defense.

Independence comes in stages like everything else. Let's look at it this way:

a) If you were a highly skilled technical person with a salary of say 50K, you would be, in a sense, independent. Why? Because if you ever felt the need to leave the company, your high level of skilled training would make it rather easy for you to get as good a job or an even better one somewhere else. Being Black and highly skilled could in certain situations make it even easier to move to another spot. In other situations, probably most, being Black would make it more difficult.

     b) If you were in business for yourself, you would probably be more independent of an authority figure (boss) than you would be in any type of job. But you would be more dependent on other types of people, namely employees, customers, bankers, suppliers, etc.

     c) If you were involved in more than one business, you would be free from worry (independent) over having to succeed in any one business under any one set of circumstances.

     d) If you had savings, investments, assets and credit, you would be much freer from concern (but in no sense totally free) of being threatened to change your interests or lifestyle due to the slowdown of your businesses. Independence means being able to lose a great deal of wealth over a specified period of time and still be able to do most, if not all of the things you like to do anyway. Finally, independence means that you have so many assets at your hand that you can shift, reverse and adjust to an almost unlimited number of new or changing situations.

11. WEALTH IS RELATED TO THE OPPORTUNITY TO EXPRESS THE CREATIVE URGES.

     I believe that there are millions and millions of people who have a deep desire to explore and develop their creative talents. Some would like to learn to play the piano or other instruments. Others would like to paint, design and sew, act, write or compose. Some folks see physical activity as the outlet for their creative urge so they play tennis, swim, jog, play golf or lift weights. Ninety-nine percent of the time people will say that they cannot *afford* to do these creative hobbies more often than they do. They usually mean that they do not have the time to give to their hobby or that they do not have the money to buy what is needed to participate more fully in their hobby. One of the best ways to tell if a person is wealthy is to see if they are doing what they want to do. The reason we say that rich White men play golf on the weekdays is because White men like to play golf on the weekdays, but only the wealthy ones can afford to do it.

12. *WEALTH IS RELATED TO SHARING.*

"Giving is better than receiving," is a popular phrase. I wonder if the originator of that phrase was rich or poor. I don't wonder if it applies to everyone because I believe it does. Poor folks suffer not only because they do not have themselves, but they suffer because they are denied the joy of giving to others as well. How many poor folks ached because they could not afford to give their children, parents, and grandparents things that they wanted, needed and deserved. Some poor folks suffer agony over accepting handouts. Others suffer greater agony seeing loved ones (whom they believe they should be able to help) having to accept handouts also. Wealth means abundance, and when there is abundance, there can be much sharing and therefore much happiness. Show me a person who cannot afford to share, and I will show you a poor man, even if a millionaire.

This concludes the discussion on the definition of wealth, and I hope you can see that wealth is a lot more than how much a person makes per week or year. It is important that this point is very clear to all people who are interested in becoming wealthy. You can only go after something after you are clear about what it is and how it relates to other important things. Many people have actually gained wealth but were unhappy because they did not understand what has just been laid out to you in the preceding pages.

Becoming wealthy is largely a process of developing opportunities, looking for opportunities and taking full advantage of opportunities when they finally do come along. If all a person looks for is a better job, they will probably never become a wealthy person.

At various points in this book we will ask you to forget salary altogether and concentrate on understanding all the other avenues to wealth. For example, rather than asking, "What is my salary for the year?" you may ask yourself:

1. How much tax shelter can be gained this year?
2. How much equity (dollar value stored in an asset) can be gained this year?
3. How much credit can I gain this year?
4. How much refinancing can I arrange this year?
5. How much can I save this year?
6. How much knowledge and money making skills can I learn this year?
7. How many sales can I make this year?

It is the development of all the avenues toward wealth that leads to wealth. Now that we *do* have a better understanding of wealth, we will now turn our attention to the wealthy folks themselves to see how they did it. Most things in this life work on a set of principles, and once you understand the principles, you can do just about anything. When man wanted to build machines that could fly, he studied the birds and the principles they used to fly. He applied those principles to the machines and the machines now fly, taking us with it.

The rich (I call them Fortune Builders) seem to follow certain principles also. Obviously, nobody follows all the principles all the time, but I don't think that that is important. If you can apply even half of the principles outlined in the next chapter, I guarantee you'll find yourself moving closer to your financial goals.

Common Characteristics
of Fortune Builders

It would seem fairly logical that if a person truly wanted to build a large income and live a very comfortable lifestyle, then he or she would study the habits and the techniques of the rich to see how fortunes are made. White folks can study and do study the rich because, among other reasons, there are so very many rich White folks in America to study. White youth can gain tons of insight, encouragement and inspiration from the broad spectrum of America's successful professionals, businessmen, artists and politicians. Black folks, on the other hand, have a much smaller number of success stories and visable role models to emulate and the spectrum of fields is not in any way nearly as broad. Today the Black folks who make the media are still largely athletes, musicians or comedians. Left almost totally out of any kind of coverage are the few among us who have made a mark in business, manufacturing, science or law.

The worse part of this great difference in the numbers and types of racial role models is not the perpetuation of the old racist stereotype, but the tremendous apathy and cynicism that develop among Black folks. Black folks often "cop an attitude." The attitudes often are:

1) There is nothing that the common Black man can do to improve his economic position unless he's some type of athlete or singer or highly educated professional. (Note: many professionals aren't making any real money either).

OR

2) White folks can do anything and get over and rich without paying any dues.

OR

3) All White folks do is hold the Black man down.

A most popular attitude seems to be that:

4) Education and hard work are useless. One may as well be cool, lay back and do only enough "to get over" because it "don't make no difference no how." The White man's in power and he ain't giving nothing up.

All of these attitudes kill the hope, desire and the spirit to struggle for a better existence. Black folks become so convinced that they are powerless that they, in fact, can often be observed doing absolutely nothing.

Such attitudes are perfectly reasonable and understandable given the tremendous efforts Black folks have historically made to get ahead in this country. The continued backsliding and backstabbing response of the greater society would kill the will of most normal people, Black or White.

White folks do have it easier getting over in America and probably will continue to do so for quite some time. What you, my frustrated reader, (and you have a right to be frustrated) need to understand is that *there is a method* to getting over in America. If you are serious about improving your condition, you must dedicate yourself to learning the methods and applying them daily. There will be sacrifices, a casting off of old habits and a taking on of new habits as you make the transition from poverty to comfort. In one word, it will mean *change,* a lot of change, and for most people that is difficult.

Because you are Black, you will have to use a little more of your physical, emotional and intellectual strengths to master the money making methods of this country. You really have very little choice.

The principles explained in this chapter and pretty much throughout the book apply to the Fortune *Builder* and not to the old rich families in America. It is important to be clear from the beginning that there are definite differences in the actions and habits between those who happened to have been born rich and those who started with little and built their own fortune. There will be a lot of generalizing here and many may well claim that there are many broad sweeping statements. This is necessary because we are focusing on general wealth building principles and not individual case studies. Obviously, many may be able to name some persons who did not travel the route suggested here. I will contend that these people are exceptions rather than the rule. If all this is clear, let us now examine the common characteristics of the Fortune Builders. These characteristics are not necessarily listed in any type of order, but when a very key characteristic is listed, I try to point it out.

FORTUNE BUILDERS HAVE SUCCESS ORIENTED ATTITUDES

There will be many, many factors that will help determine your successes and failures in this life. Some you will have no control over at all while others will be a direct result of your plannning, work and creativity. Of all the factors outlined in this chapter, I believe that none is as important as one's individual attitude about one's work and life in general. Attitudes, it seems, determine everything.

In all of the how-to books on the market today (how to diet, make love, relieve stress, etc.), there is usually a section dedicated to a discussion of attitudes. I have read many of these passages and have found them too weak, simplistic, and as far as the Black experience is concerned, irrelevant. I would like to take a new approach here and discuss attitudes in three parts. Part one involves looking at our introduction to the idea of attitudes. Part two is an examination of where we are now: our present attitudes. Part three concerns what we have to do: attitudes which are needed to take us to our goals.

Most of us, if we think about it, had a negative experience with the word *attitude*. In elementary school if we were talkers, playful, cocky or a bit different from our classmates, we were told by our teacher that she did *not like our attitude*. Throughout our school years other teachers, principals or athletic coaches scolded us or reported to our parents that if we wanted to stay in school or do well in school, that *we had better change our attitude*. After high school, Black men especially were subject to low-level jobs, the military or sometimes prison. At each point a designated person, whether a sergeant or captain in the service, a foreman or supervisor at the job site, or the warden or jailer in the prison system, was there to remind us that if we didn't straighten up our *attitude* and do as we were told that somebody was going to make life miserable for us. Thus, to Black folks, and I suspect to many White folks as well, the word attitude reminds us of some form of authority figure trying to dominate our lives. Someone, from our parents to the jailer, was standing over us demanding—forcing us to submit to their rules and their idea of how we should act or be or think. On the whole there were but two things one could do under these circumstances: either submit and fall into the mold that some other persons or institution had designed for us or rebel and say, "To hell with everybody; I'm going to do what I want to do."

Today most of us are still pretty much in one bag or the other. One bag of folks has traveled the straight and narrow. They got good grades, went off to college and now hold a decent job. They feel that they did most of the right things, but somehow at 25 or 30 years old they ran out of steam because they didn't know who to ask what to do next. They never actually made their own decision; thus, they feel alone, nervous, generally lost and lacking in confidence.

The other bag is that of the Black rebel who got so tired of being told what to do that he or she just programmed himself or herself to be against almost everything. They may have done their own thing for the last few years or so, but they too are somewhat lost and they realize that they don't have much to show for what they've been doing the last few years.

And so here we are 27, 30 or 35 years old and ready to do something with our lives, but not quite sure what it is. I know; I understand because I've been there.

I will give you now some idea of the attitudes that other financially successful people have adopted, and you determine how you can apply them to your situation.

1. *FORTUNE BUILDERS THINK BIG.*

How does one who has always thought small begin to think big? Try this. If you are twenty years old and work until you retire at sixty-five years old, you will likely make at least half a million dollars in your lifetime. If you have a really nice job, say $16,000 yearly, you will probably make three-quarters of a million dollars in your lifetime. Now those are big sums of money, aren't they? Think about what you want to buy with that one-half to three-quarters of a million dollars. Believe it or not, if you followed your normal buying and earning habits you will most likely be poor at sixty-five years old like almost all other retired salaried employees, Black and White, in this country. Think about it. The old made their bundle too, but they are poor now and will be so until death. Why? Because first they didn't build anything along the way; they simply earned and spent. Secondly, a half million, even three-quarters of a million dollars is not that much money stretched out over 35-45 years. Thus, you need to think big. You need to think in terms of sums over a million dollars, and you're going to have to think about *building something* such as a business, a practice or a series of profitable investments.

2. *FORTUNE BUILDERS DO NOT THINK IN TERMS OF FAILURE.*

Let me draw a way out comparison in order to make a point. If you started out by car to drive from New York to Los Angeles and found yourself one night sleeping in a hick town in Ohio where there was bad food, nothing to do and terrible hotels, you wouldn't panic would you? Of course not because you know that you would only be staying in that town for one night and you'd probably never have to pass through there again. After a good night's sleep you hit the road again *on your way to California.* That is the way Fortune Builders feel about so-called failure. They don't panic because they look at failure as simply a necessary stopping-off point *on their way to the* goal. The only way you would panic in the hick town in Ohio is if some mysterious force forced you to stay there and accept it as home. But you couldn't imagine what kind of force that would be, could you? Likewise, the Fortune Builder would only panic at so-called failure if some mysterious force forced him or her to accept that particular failure as *the end*. But he or she, like you, could not possibly imagine what kind of force that would be. Fortune Builders learn from so-called failures, not give in to them. It's part of their attitude.

3. *FORTUNE BUILDERS SET THEIR OWN PACE IN THEIR MARCH TOWARD FORTUNE.*

Fortune Builders, like the rebels, do not like someone telling them what they can and cannot do. It doesn't mean that they break laws; it just means that they might skip certain steps and bullshit along the way to their goal. Life is full of thousands of little security guards saying "you can't do A before you do B," "you can't get past here without an appointment," etc. Fortune Builders understand very early that a lot of so-called barriers are just bull. They learn how to *cut through* the bull, leap frogging over the stupid who stand and wait in line (to receive their bull). Their attitude is that if they are smart enough to get around a hurdle to save time and energy, why not do it regardless of what everybody else is doing or is told to do.

4. *FORTUNE BUILDERS ASSUME FULL RESPONSIBILITY FOR THEIR DEFEATS AND VICTORIES.*

If you were to ask successful people why they were successful, many of them would come on real humble and modest and say things like, "I had good parents" or "good luck," or "right place at the right time" and other bull. But if you asked them in private, away from the crowd, they would probably say, "Because I worked my ass off and I was determined not to take no for an answer." Most people believe they deserve the success that they have received. Why? Because Fortune Builders are more aware than anybody else of the risks, sacrifices and work that led them to where they are. They had always assumed full responsibility of having to know (or find out) what to do, whom to see, what to say, how to do it, when to do it, how long to do it, etc. Most successful people travel a lonely road, and if they do not do what needs to be done, it will not get done. They have to be the originator, planner and performer. They then count the money when the show is over. They blame nobody for their failures other than themselves. They have adopted the attitude of independence and responsibility.

With Black folks, however, there is and has always been the problem of racism. Black folks do not have the opportunity to fail or succeed strictly on the basis of their own brains, ideas, work and sacrifice. All too often White power intercedes and destroys Black work and productivity for no other reason than the fact that it is Black.

A very important question that any Black person needs to ask him or herself in the examination of their own attitude is "How do you deal with racism? How do you continue to have a positive determined attitude when it appears that the more powerful forces in this country seem dedicated to seeing you fail? How do you deal with that?"

To that I say this: For every man and woman, there are factors internally which he or she *can* control and external factors which he or she *cannot* control. Racism is an external factor in American life which no one person can change. But any person can greatly *influence* the way the world responds to them as an individual. Once persons learn and *master themselves* and learn to control all the *internal* aspects of their life, that they do have some control over (such as the use of their time, money, brains, emotions, work, etc.), they will find that they do have substantial control on how the outside world responds and reacts to them. That idea or principle applies to Black folks as well as White, although not to the same degree. What is a star? A star is someone who has gained fame (maybe fortune also) for having done one or more things in such a way that it merits attention or publicity. A star has used his or her abilities, the internal factors in his or her life which they have some control over, to do something noteworthy. But something else happens also. The world reacts to the star differently than when he or she was just "a *person."* The star gets special courtesy, is listened to and gets access to all kinds of favors and opportunities that he or she did not have access to before. Why? Because of the principle that I mentioned above—when you do something with the internally controlled factors of your life, you can force the outside world to react differently to you. America is a nation of hero worshippers and everybody loves a star, any kind of star. Stars don't get attention because they demand it; they get it because the public likes giving it to them.

While acknowledging that poverty, ignorance and racism exist, Black folks must look past that and assume the full responsibility for what we do with our lives and not use anything as a crutch or excuse to hold us back. You may not be able to achieve all that you could or should have, but you have enough control over so many things in your life that you could literally *force yourself* to get to a lot of places that you do want to go.

5. *FORTUNE BUILDERS MAKE MANY, MANY QUICK DECISIONS*

One attitude that stops a lot of people from accomplishing anything is one where they can never make up their mind about what they want to do when they have to make a decision. Because they can't make up their mind, they often do nothing which is the same thing as making up our mind to do nothing. You cannot go anywhere in this life by doing nothing. Fortune Builders are interested in quick progress. In order to make quick progress, you must do many things, and in order to do many things, you have to make many decisions. To make many decisions you have to learn to make quick decisions.

How does one learn how to make quick decisions? Simple. When a decision has to be made, you figure out what it costs in money, time, effort, responsibility, etc. Then you figure out the probable benefits for that decision and figure out if the benefit is worth the cost. Finally, you ask yourself, "What is the worse thing that can possibly go wrong and is it worth the risk? Will I be able to deal with the outcome if the worse does happen? How will I deal with the outcome if the worse happens? Will the cost of dealing with the outcome be too great considering the possible reward if everything goes right?" After you answer each of the questions, you make your decision. In the beginning this process may take a long time; but, like everything else, you get faster and better by repeating the process over and over again. Pretty soon your mind will be so clear about what has to be done to get you where you are trying to go that decisions will be automatic.

Making decisions has a lot to do with two ideas that we hear a lot about: confidence and enthusiasm. What is confidence? Confidence is the internal peace you feel in knowing that the decisions you have made and the direction that you are heading in are right for you and you are in control. When do you get confidence in yourself? You get confidence when you look at all the hundreds of little decisions you have made, sum them all up and determine that you made more good ones than bad ones. If you didn't make more good ones than bad ones, then at least you learned a lot about how to make better decisions. It is at that point that you will begin to gain confidence in yourself and your ability to make a decision. But you must start somewhere, sometime to *make* decisions and you must *carry out* your decisions. Otherwise you will have no list of decisions to analyze, and you will still lack confidence. Clear?

Where does enthusiasm come from? Enthusiasm comes from seeing, hearing and feeling your goals coming closer and closer to your grasp. As you become aware that your idea, vision or goal is now getting to be much more a reality and that you can almost predict when it will come true, you will probably be experiencing this feeling we call enthusiasm. But like confidence, enthusiasm requires you to work persistently towards something; otherwise, there will be nothing to be enthusiastic about. I feel sorry for Black folks who play heavily into the number of lottery systems in this country. What they are really saying is, "Even though I have absolutely no control over the selection of the number and I realize my chances of winning are thousands and thousands to one, I can still have more faith and enthusiasm using this route to fortune than I would counting on my own skills and work." Would lottery gamblers say this? Never in a million years.

In summary, Fortune Builders make many fast decisions everyday and gain more confidence, enthusiasm and, as a result, wealth everyday.

6. *FORTUNE BUILDERS HAVE A CLEAR CONSCIOUS ABOUT MAKING AND HAVING A LOT OF MONEY.*

You know the Black community has so very many contradictions that sometimes you don't know whether to laugh, cry or go stark raving mad. The attitude that the Black community has toward money is rather contradictory. Let's examine it.

On one hand the Black community is poor, and many, many problems can be traced to this poverty. Under many conditions Black people will unite and acknowledge that we need more money, we deserve more money and we demand more money. It makes perfect sense that if you have a *money* problem, you get more money and solve your problem.

On the other hand, there is a lot of suspicion and doubt in the Black community given to those who actively pursue wealth. If a person wants to live well and does something more than work a nine to five job and watch television, he or she risks being given a label such as being "money crazy" or being described as "someone who only cares about money." The reasoning for this may be as follows:

Black folks have a long history of being economically exploited in this country. Traditionally, Whites have put in motion huge profit-making undertakings with scores or hundreds of underpaid or overworked laborers who were in many instances Black. After the undertaking completed its cycle, whether it was raising cotton or producing factory goods the owners received huge profits and the workers received peanut wages. In the minds of many Black folks this vicious cycle has been repeated so many times that many think it is *the only way* that money is made. To many, the idea of a person seeking to make a lot of money generates the idea of that person exploiting and misusing many innocent people. In many minds the one (making money) automatically means the intention of doing the latter (exploiting, overworking and misusing others). As a response to these perceptions, Black voices come out of the woodwork giving you extreme doubts as to the wisdom of seeking financial security and comfort for your family. You will hear people say, "money isn't everything," "money can't buy you happiness," "you can't take it with you," etc. All of these statements are designed to make you question the morality of making money. It was as if making money was sinful. Indeed,

many will quickly remind you that "money is the root of all evil," imply-
ing that those who choose to make money are themselves bound to end
up in some kind of devilish enterprise. As if these two very contradictory
attitudes were not causing enough confusion in the Black community,
our doomsday money forecasters end up being hero and superstar worshippers themselves. They love the fine clothes Diana Ross wore on her
t.v. special or the fine house Redd Foxx lives in or the car collection of
Isaac Hayes that they saw in some magazine. They love Ali, not only
because he's handsome and a winner, but because he's rich as well. They
like to see their champion, the peoples' champ, ride a long limousine,
stay in the best hotels around the world and otherwise live like a king.
But you, the man in the street who believes that you are entitled to at
least some of that high living, are to be watched and preached at regarding
the evils of money. Does it all make sense? Of course not. But many
Black folks do not struggle to live the good life because they do not
believe they have a right to live well. The society has programmed him or
her that only the "stars" deserve to taste the wealth that all of our ancestors died to create.

Let's face it. Nobody is giving money away to America's Black folks
—not other Black Americans because they do not have it to give and
not White Americans as they are still highly influenced by their own
racism. This being the case, getting rich in America will not be easy for
any minority. For some to attempt to do so while wrestling with all these
contradicting feelings about money will totally destroy their efforts. Fortune Builders do not and cannot afford to labor under any kind of guilt
in insuring comfort, security and independence for his immediate and
extended families. If you are serious about making money, then your
attitude must be one of a clear conscience or you'll sink before you swim.

7. FORTUNE BUILDERS DON'T GIVE A DAMN WHAT PEOPLE SAY.

The world is full of talented people of all races, income levels and
beliefs who have never produced up to their capability for reasons that
have nothing to do with racism, lack of opportunity or money. Quite
simply, many people are highly influenced by the remarks, criticisms,
opinions, judgments and advice that others give them. A person can
have a talent and a desire to use that talent and be on his or her way to
success when suddenly an ignorant negative force enters his or her life and
kills enthusiasm, confidence and finally desire itself. This is a tragedy, and
unfortunately Black folks suffer more discouragement than others simply

because there is more doubt, ignorance and negativism in poverty neighborhoods and areas. Often this discouragement comes from an unexpected source: a mother, father, sister or brother. "Close" friends or relatives call themselves doing you a favor by advising you on a more practical way of living. They would like to see you "come down off the cloud," "stop dreaming" and lead a normal life of college, job, family and so on.

Fortune Builders, Whites as well as Blacks, have to learn to ignore negative forces, negative people and generally unsupportive elements until they are in a position to judge for themselves the possibility of their ventures.

The people who really catch hell from critics are the really brilliant, innovative, and original thinkers and doers. This is because most people have a problem with a new idea or a new direction unless it's wrapped, packaged and sold through some commercial means. An untried, untested, unpopular point of view will draw unsolicited, negative comments every time. Understand this if you understand nothing else in this book: *There is a very, very thin line between being a genius and being called stark raving crazy, between being the world's biggest loser and its biggest winner.* Let me explain:

> Every school age child that has any interest in science knows that Thomas Edison invented the light bulb. What they didn't learn in school is that before Mr. Edison successfully selected the right strip of metal to carry the electrical current to create light, that he had tried *ten thousand other combinations of metals in exactly the same way, and failed.* Now, picture for one moment what the masses of people could have said about Edison if they knew what he was trying to do. Surely he would have been thought to be a madman. And even those who would have been supportive would have thought the man crazy after the first thousand failures. Instead, Edison succeeded and went from being crazy to being heralded as the genius of the twentieth century (along with Albert Einstein who was also ridiculed for putting forth a theory which nobody else could believe or understand).

Black folks have been told for decades what they couldn't do or at least what they shouldn't try to do. There is an absence of faith in Black folks' capabilities on the part of not only White folks but other Black folks as well. As a Fortune Builder you have to block out the bad or negative vibes that will surely come your way. You will be accused of being cocky, a know-it-all and other things once your detractors find that you are not taking their advice. Regardless of what is said or who says it, you have to adopt the attitude of "to hell with what people say unless they have *taken the time* to understand what you are trying to do, why you are trying to do it, and/or offer a better way to help you do it." Otherwise, to hell with them, and that may include your mama!

8. *FORTUNE BUILDERS PROGRAM AND MOTIVATE THEM-SELVES.*

All of us are programmed in many, many ways, from television, radio, newspapers, magazines, billboard signs, and a thousand other sources we get suggestions of what to believe in. For a person to live in America and believe that he or she is not affected by its mass advertising and computer programming is a little naive to say the least. The nation's programming is aimed primarily at Mr. Average Guy or, better still, Mr. Average White Guy. My Average Guy has an average job, average house and average ambitions and goals. What that means to you, the Fortune Builder, is that America's programming is not designed for you because you have no intention of being Mr. Average Guy. Once you decide to become a Fortune Builder, you need to design a program for yourself to help you on your journey. You need to include in your programming material that which will motivate you and give you an emotional or intellectually stimulating experience for those times when you find yourself puzzled, discouraged and doubtful of reaching your goal. Everyone experiences down moments, even the most positive thinking persons. This idea is discussed in the last chapter.

REVIEW OF SUCCESS ORIENTED ATTITUDES

I hope you can see from the preceding pages why it is so very important for a person to give a lot of attention and focus on their attitudes. Black folks must develop attitudes that allow them to be open to information and inspection that will help project them forward toward their goal. At the same time attitudes must be developed which close out all the negative forces coming from friends, foes and family.

Briefly, success oriented attitudes are:

1) Thinking big. You are an important person with a lot to do and a lot to gain. Your mind is thinking in terms of millions of dollars over your lifetime.

2) Accepting Failure as only temporary pauses in your quest for your goal. They can be extremely useful in helping you to figure out how to do your thing better, faster and with more determination.

3) Setting your own pace in your march to fortune. Don't let any number of security guard thinking people tell you how fast or how slow you should go to get where you want to go. Your job is to handle the obstacles, skip steps when appropriate, and always cut through the bull.

4) Assuming the full responsibility of getting the job done. You will eventually get much help and encouragement as you draw closer to your goals and it becomes obvious to everyone that you will reach it. But until that time comes, however, you have to make sure that you understand that if you want something done, do it yourself. It is nobody's job to make you a fortune. If you don't do it, it won't get done.

5) Learning how to make many fast decisions. In time you will build up a great reserve of confidence, knowledge and enthusiasm, all the factors needed to push you to your goal.

6) Having a clear conscious about the value of making and keeping money. Money is not evil; it is freedom, independence and the ability to help those that you choose to help.

7) Having the ability to ignore the doubts and negative opinions of others and having the strength to keep on pushing while being surrounded by disagreeable elements.

8) Having the ability to design a programming and motivational package that helps you move forward rather than preparing you to settle for what Mr. Average Guy wants.

With a full understanding of these ideas on attitudes, we can now explain the other twenty odd characteristics that identify those in the money.

2. FORTUNE BUILDERS TAKE RISKS.

There is an old expression which says "nothing ventured nothing gained." Unfortunately, like many other sayings, people just mouth the words and really do not understand or apply the true meaning of what's being offered as advice.

There is tremendous competition in America for the dollar bill, and if there was some safe, secure and easy way of collecting them, I'm sure everybody would be rich. But there is no prescribed or guaranteed route to riches, and it results in quite a bit of uncertainty (called risk) for all who pursue fame and fortune. Obviously this is even truer if you are a Black American.

Most people don't have to wrestle with the fear, the loneliness and the risk of doing one's own thing. They get enough enjoyment and pleasure by simply talking about it or watching others. What most people actually do is to eventually settle on a modest paying, secure job that allows them to feel like a productive person in the society. They hope for some good luck or some future motivation (later on down the line) to push them towards a good income. If such luck or motivation does not occur, then the emphasis usually sways back to security and they use the rest of their working life to hold on to what they have.

A Fortune Builder makes the decision somewhere along this boring series of events to take a risk and fall out of line with the general masses. Some idea, vision or goal pushes and tests him or her and forces him or her to put himself or herself on the line. Risk becomes the order of the day and probably for the rest of their lives. He or she is almost always in a position to lose what he or she has built, but he or she takes that chance anyway.

    a) Stable Income. They risk the idea of knowing for "sure" that they will always receive from their JOB a minimum amount of dollars per week to take care of their family's needs. This income furnishes a strong psychological contentment and the idea of risking it or giving it up often affects a person more mentally than it actually would financially. Almost all Fortune Builders eventually give up the so-called secure jobs.

    b) Stored Savings. Savings represents years of work and accomplishment. The idea of risking that financial cushion by spending it on some untried venture is a real test of one's willingness to take on a risk.

    c) Loved-One's Money. Many businesses were started on Dad's money, father-in-law's money, auntie's or grandma's money. Having the guts to ask a close relative or friend, who is not likely to be wealthy themselves, to lend (give) you their money so you can try out this idea you have is a stronger sense of risk than using your own money.

    d) A Good Marriage. Many marriages have come apart because one mate wanted to quit his or her job and rely solely on their own enterprise for a livelihood. This idea to most folks represents a risk far greater than losing anybody's money and has stopped many a dreamer or Fortune Builder dead in his or her tracks. Hopefully, as a Fortune Builder you have the ability to sell your mate on the potential of your venture. If not . . . you have a heavy decision to make.

e) Wasted Time and Effort. Everyone will run out of time and energy (life) before he or she runs out of money. In a sense your time and energy is even more important than money at some point. A Fortune Builder realizes this also but is willing to put forth the risk of wasted effort and time in order to pursue his/her thing.

f) Ego or Reputation. Fortune Builders usually have tremendous egos. Usually their earlier educational or career success in life "proved" to them that they were indeed special or gifted persons destined to be famous or among the elite. The idea that their peers could ever be in a position to ridicule them for failure is absolutely terrifying. Thus, often the biggest simple thing at risk to the fortune hunter is their own name and self image. Every Fortune Builder gives at least a passing thought to the "What will they say" syndrome.

Every major item at risk in the quest to do one's own thing is a heavy. Every Fortune Builder, to some extent, is aware of these weighty considerations and many others which have not been mentioned. After agonizing over all the possibilities of what "might" happen, they decide to plan ahead and "do it."

3. FORTUNE BUILDERS HAVE A VISION.

All Fortune Builders experience a vision of what they desire to become. Long before they achieve success, in any common sense of the word, they see the series of events happening in their brain. Often they fall short or surpass this vision of themselves. One thing is clear, however, and that is, that in their vision they see themselves in a much different, much better set of circumstances than they presently find themselves.

Question: What is the difference between a dream and a vision?

A dream is what happens when you go to sleep. You see yourself in a dream in a nice house, but you don't know where it is or how you got there. You have other nice possessions, but their origin is also a mystery. Things are happening to you but their origin is also a mystery. Things are happening to you but you are not doing too much in the way of action yourself. You are surrounded by a number of people whom you do not know. In short, dreams are a mystery in the sense that you can offer no explanation of why or what happened. The whole thing was not a consciously controlled act anyway, and the actual substance of a dream is half forgotten when you are in your "right mind!" That is a dream. Dreaming can *lead to* a vision, especially as you try to wrestle with the meaning of your dreams.

A vision is a perfected image of the future. You see yourself in a highly developed state brought about by work and struggle. If you are into music, you see yourself as a master of your instrument. If you are into sports, you see in your mind your own body dunking the basketball, socking the homerun or scoring the touchdown. Your possessions are not mysteriously there but are the product of your success. The people around you are the people of your choosing because you are where you want to be and working with individuals who complement your efforts. In short, your vision is your plans brought to live action in your mind. Anything short of this vision will leave your plans as a series of statements in your head or a series of sentences on a white piece of paper.

There are other basic differences between a vision and a dream:

a) A vision is repeated constantly in your brain by your own will. You continually bring forth the image to see if there are any changes that you want to make. You then alter your vision as is necessary. A dream can be repeated but you are not in a position to will or not will it into being, and often it changes many times in significant ways.

b) A vision serves a definite purpose. It determines the *ideal* to which you are striving.

My task here is to show you how to make money. A long time before the money is actually made it happens in your brain. You see it in color and panavision on the silver screen in your mind. The first question that will be answered in your mind is *what* will you do that will allow you to make all this money. That is the question that every single Fortune Builder has to ask and answer. Everything else comes afterwards. Do not be dismayed if you have to adjust, change or even reverse your (plans) visions. The important thing is that the big picture is up there on the screen of your mind.

4. *FORTUNE BUILDERS ARE ENERGETIC.*

Fortune Builders are almost always very energetic, active people. It is an absolute necessity. Many people believe that they lack the necessary energy and drive to get ahead in life and thus never attempt to do too much more than the daily routine. Before you discount your energy level, however, let's be clear about where the energy of these human dynamos comes from.

a) Love. Love is by far the greatest source of energy for the person moving ahead. It is easy for people to put a lot of time, energy, attention and emotion into something they love. In a racist society limiting many Blacks to jobs that no one else is interested in, energy is drained rather than generated. Black people are forced to grab what is available to eat and support their families. The idea of liking what you are doing seldom enters into the picture. But every person serious about making money almost always *has to find* something that he or she truly would like to do. This country is extremely big and there are many ways to get in touch with things that are not on your doorsteps or in your community. When you find something that excites you, something that you can grow to love, you will have tapped a gigantic vein of energy within your system.

b) Success. The accomplishment of one thing can often lead to the desire to attempt to do something else more difficult. This cycle is rather easy to understand. It is quite common to see people tremendously successful in one thing venture off into another altogether different field. The positive egotistical and physical feedback from succeeding in something can trigger a rush of energy that can often be stopped only after the body and mind are truly exhausted. This is seen all the time in athletic events and live music concerts.

It is important to understand that people may use their energy level to become successful, but then being successful gives a tremendous boost to their energy level too.

c) Physical Fitness. Energy comes from the ability of the body to generate it. It stands to reason that the better condition your equipment is in the better it will work. The decade of the 70's is when concern for the condition of the human body reached a peak. Diet books made a permanent residence atop national best seller lists. Barbells, exercise mats and sit-up boards sold like ice cream. And there was jogging. Jogging, jogging and more jogging was the order of the day along with tennis, racketball and health spas. Why all this concern over the human body? There are many, many reasons, but one of the major reasons was the desire for more pep and energy. The human body is a fantastic mechanism. Push it more and it will give you more. The greatest "health nut" in the world would never have imagined 11 to 14 thousand people lining up to run twenty-six miles through New York City's streets. Millions more can run five to ten miles or do a couple hundred sit-ups, push-ups or whatever. A Fortune Builder seeking more energy for his or her enterprises would do well to start and maintain some sort of exercise program.

d) Sense of Responsibility. Imagine the following:

A man starts a business which does very well making him a lot of money. The business grows and the owner involves a lot of the people who had supported and encouraged him so that they too can get a part of the big payoff. Difficulties develop and the business falls on hard times. It seems the owner has to work twice as hard to make the same amount of money. Where does the energy come from? It comes from the *pressure* of knowing that many wonderful people would suffer if he, the owner, didn't go the extra mile to insure success. The energy comes from the *fear* that if he didn't work double time, he too would have to go back begging for his old job to support his family.

Energy can thus be generated from negative sources of influence as well as positive ones. It's called *running scared*, and many Fortune Builders used this source of energy to get them over the hump and out into the big money.

There are many sources of energy boosters and they can produce general and consistent high levels of performance, or they can produce great peaks as in life-threatening situations. Sooner or later, however, all Fortune Builders have to rely on the greatest source of all energy—sheer will power. At some point when all else fails and you have a task to be done, one has to simply learn how to use one's mind to push yourself through the required number of movements. Sooner or later if you give your interest enough of your time and the interest is maintained, all the various sources of energy will impact on you at once. When this happens, you too will be the human dynamo that you have observed in others.

5. *FORTUNE BUILDERS HAVE A MONEY CONSCIOUSNESS.*

In this world you do not get something without going after it, at least not when you're Black. For sure you will not get money unless and until you put the idea in your mind . . . constantly. Let me make an illustration.

Have you ever seen anybody who was extremely overweight? They tried diets, a few sit-ups and hypnosis, but nothing lasted or worked very long. The person blew right back up again, right? Well, poverty is like being overweight; you save a little here and win a lottery or horse race there, catch a sale here and there, but in the final analysis you are still very poor. What is needed to change these situations? I'll tell you what is needed —extreme action which can only be brought about by a change of mind.

In a fat person's life he or she may come across the extreme indignity, the turning point, that mental or physical pain that hits nerves so deep as to change the consciousness of our overeater. What happens after the decision is made to reduce once and for all is that that person watches *everything*, and I mean *everything*, that they eat. They learn the caloric content of three hundred portions of food by memory and watch every morsel that they put in their mouth. That, my friend, is extreme. Their friends may compliment them on their new figure on one hand but lose their desire to visit or go out with them on the other hand because of their excessive concern about what's on the menu or how the food is being cooked. Now our fat friend may loose seventy-five or a hundred pounds; but unless they actually change certain aspects of their life, there is no assurance that they will not gain it back. Thus, they may be forced into a kind of partial diet the rest of their lives. This rule is the *extremism is needed for modest gain* rule. What this says is that sometimes one has to take things to an extreme in order to make only modest progress because of the sheer weight of all the forces and factors going against you. Many people do not like to appear extreme. They want to appear "normal," "ok" or "like everybody else," etc. Many would rather suffer the problems that they are suffering rather than take drastic action to correct it. Everyone has to make this decision for themselves.

What does this have to do with money making? Everything. Money consciousness is just a variation of diet consciousness except rather than thinking of food and what not to eat everyday you think of money and how to make it every single day. This may sound like no big thing. But try it and watch what happens to your relationships when you become known as the "cheapskate" or "money lover."

The major question is could you maintain your money consciousness if your family and friends tried to make you feel guilty about it? Would you be one of those Fortune Builders who succeeded because you thought about it and *acted on it every day*? Or would you be back at the homestead drinking wine with the rest of the party showing how much of a regular guy you were? This decision, like all the others, is yours to make.

6. *FORTUNE BUILDERS HAVE A VALUE FOR KNOWLEDGE.*

The people who make money in America generally have a basic understanding of money areas of life and commerce. Some of these areas include sales, marketing, advertising, accounting, law, human psychology, real estate, tax, and many other important sources of information. As the national and international economic situation gets more complicated and as the competition for the dollar gets tougher, Fortune Builders develop an even higher appreciation for study and analysis. Naturally the Fortune Builder does not shoulder all the weight for knowing all that must be known to run their enterprise successfully. There are experts to be hired for specific purposes and at the proper time. The Fortune Builders realize that sufficient knowledge and information is absolutely necessary to make the best use of energy, ideas and money.

In the Black community, there is a tendency to confuse knowledge with formal training or college degrees. American educational institutions are seldom developed to pass along practical information. Most instructors get their information from old books rather than recent real life experience. What all of this means is that most people interested in making money have to educate themselves on the important areas of knowledge they will need to understand. In order the develop your own educational program you must have a value for information to begin with. You must see a direct connection between the time spent in learning a new subject and your growth in your ability to produce income. If you ever spend much time reading about successful people, you will almost always see where they make a claim of having educated themselves. In almost all cases this is probably the truth, and you will have to learn to do the same. Your greatest amount of income-producing activity will probably take place between your twenty-fifth and fiftieth birthdays. Your greatest amount of reading, study and self-education should take place during this time period also.

7. FORTUNE BUILDERS WORK HARD.

Fortune Builders work hard, fast, long and smart. It is very important that it is clear that good old work is at the very center of building a fortune for anybody. That old picture of the happy-go-lucky White man on a golf course while the workers toil at the machines is a common image in the minds of many Black folks. Well, happy-go-lucky White men *do* play golf on weekdays by the thousands all across America. But most of them spent years busting their butt working alone when there were no employees. They worked under the fear of failure and the pressure of production. They've had their share of nervous breakdowns, heart failure, broken marriages and all the rest. Am I trying to rally up sympathy for the boss man? No! I'm just letting you know that if *they* worked hard to get their piece of the action, what should that tell you about what you have to do?

Actually, working smart and consistently is more important than working at the grindstone everyday.

I'd like to pass along a very memorable story I heard just before I entered law school.

Al Brown, a successful Black attorney in Newark, New Jersey went to Howard Law School, an all Black law school, in the 1950's. The other students use to always make fun of how long and hard he studied for his exams . . . maybe the suggestion was that he did not have enough upstairs to get through school. He use to say, "The lights are still on at Harvard Law; it's three a.m. and the dorm lights are still on." One day a student asked him what he meant and he ran the whole thing down. Said Brown, "Look man, there are some White boys at Harvard Law who are third generation lawyers and they drive Corvettes on campus now. If they are White and I'm Black, rich and I'm poor, at Harvard and I'm at Howard, third generation lawyers and I'm first generation college and they got *their* lights burning 'til three a.m. studying, what in the hell would mine be doing off at that time."

Nuff said, I hope.

8. *FORTUNE BUILDERS ARE CREATIVE.*

I would say that with the exception of having the proper attitude, being creative is probably the next most important thing necessary to being a millionaire in this country. But we have three major problems, especially in the Black community, regarding creativity:
1) We have a school system which kills creativity early and keeps it from surfacing for the entire maturation period of young kids everywhere in the country.
2) Secondly, we have a confusion, a mystique and an apathy regarding just what creativity is.
3) And finally, we have a great problem in this country, specifically in reference to Black folks, in appreciating creativity when it does arise.

Let me explain. I would say that if I took the average person to a first or second grade class in New York City and then to another class in San Francisco, he or she could not tell much, if any, difference between the two classes. This is because the basis of education in this society is structure, order, conformity and duplication. Most first, third and fifth graders study pretty much the same things in all schools all across this country. Only in high school do most students begin to get any kind of variety in their education. Even then it usually becomes a mere choice of three or four different tracks leading to various status levels in the society. One thing this type of system does is to kill creativity because each student is taught to conform with the studies, the behavior, the dress and the performance of his or her fellow students. Without working this point into the ground, the idea is this: Creativity means new, different, innovative, untried, etc. The contradiction should be obvious. After twelve years or so you can see why young people don't even know what creativity is. This brings us to the second problem: confusion about just what creativity is.

In the school system young kids are taught that certain inventors, scientists and artists were very creative people. But they are also taught that these inventors, scientists and artists were rare geniuses. Pretty soon there is this conclusion or assumption that the only creative people are the rare geniuses and the typical student never learns that there is tremendous creative power in millions of us ordinary people as well. With an educational system that teaches conformity on one hand and the rareness of creativity on the other, it is quite easy to understand why the typical high schooler doesn't have the least bit of understanding or appreciation of their own creative abilities. Thus, the success of these students is mostly judged on their ability to conform to a model that educators themselves cannot agree on.

Finally, if, in spite of all this systemmatic brainwashing, a young person, Black or White, manages to do something really creative, all hell breaks loose. That child or person is labeled rebellious, unorthodox, weird, freaky or worse. America does not really appreciate genius oftentimes. A new thing, idea, cure, or style is ridiculed, discredited and ignored until it becomes popularized. And whose job is that? The salesman. America doesn't really love ideas; it loves salesmen. And do you know what the golden rule is among salesmen? Simple: Nothing happens until there is a sale. Think about it. The greatest ideas and gadgets in the world could be developed tomorrow, it wouldn't matter. We would all stand back, attack it, disclaim it and chastise the genius who developed it. But enter on center stage that man with shirt and tie and the broad grin, making gestures with his hands, inflections in his voice and exaggerated claims in his conversation, and we're standing in line to buy whatever it is at ridiculously high prices.

In spite of all this chaos and confusion, Fortune Builders do become creative and sell their creativity. I have a very simple idea of what creativity is. Creativity is just a twist or a turn, an adaptation or substitution that makes a concept yours. Creativity can be expressed in many ways.

a) Doing a common thing in an uncommon way.
b) Doing an uncommon thing in a common way.
c) Doing an uncommon thing in an uncommon way.

Because we are so conditioned by ideas in advertising and concerned with costs and payments of the things we like, creativity can extend to these areas as well:

d) A common thing but an uncommon promotion method.
e) An uncommon thing but a common promotion method.

f) An uncommon thing with uncommon promotion method.

g) A common thing with uncommon financing method
   (method by which customer pays for object).

h) An uncommon thing with common financing method.

i) An uncommon thing with uncommon financing method.

Let me cite some examples:

Fred is a shoeshiner. People have to climb up on a stand to have their shoes shined. Fred has a spot in a shopping area with access to electricity. One day the idea hit Fred that people really act like they're "big time" when they get their shoes shined, so he decided to give it to them with both barrels. He built a throne for his customers. He spent a couple of hundred dollars finding a large English chair, decorated it with cut glass jewels, silk and even had lights flicking on and off.

Is this silly? . . . Probably yes.

Does it create attention, curiosity and crowds? . . . Yes.

Does it create business? Yes. Does Fred make more money?

Yes, more than twice as much because he charges more money, has more customers and works longer hours. Later Fred bought an old tuxedo and drew more attention. That is an example of a common thing (shoeshine) done in an uncommon way.

EXAMPLE #2

Jane is a doctor who studied accupuncture for several years and believes in her soul that it works. Accupuncture has been in the news and many professionals have testified that it does have a scientific basis. Many people want to try it for old ills that won't go away, but they do not go out of their way to find a doctor who specialized in it. Jane realized all of this and decides to go where the people are since they won't come to her. Where are the people? Where else the mall. Jane signs a lease for a space right beside Sears in this gigantic mall in the suburbs. The other mall tenants protest because they don't think it's appropriate. Jane's attorney threatens to file suit and the resistance subsides. Now people stop buy and get their acupuncture treatment after they have done their shopping in the mall.

This is an uncommon thing (accupuncture) done in a common way (shopping mall location) and is rather creative.

EXAMPLE #3

Sometimes creativity is just common sense that other people don't seem to follow. Check out the following:

Gladys is a Black woman hell bent on making money. She owns a liquor store near the college campus and does good business. One day she heard a record that she wanted and sent a friend out to buy it. But all the record stores were closed. The idea hit her that there is almost always a close association between liquor and music. Many types of affairs start as one thing but end up as a liquor and music get-together. She thought, why not open up a record store in her liquor store? The profit would easily pay for the extra help that would be needed. So she did and a funny thing happened. People who came in to buy a record ended up buying a six pack of beer. People who came to buy liquor for a party bought new records to liven up the party. And people who never had a reason to ever come into the store before came from clear across town because it is the only *record store* open at two o'clock in the morning. Gladys made a mint. Was that creativity or common sense? How many record-liquor stores have you seen?

Anybody can learn to be creative; maybe not enough to be a genius (whatever that is) but enough to make a fortune.

In the Black community there are special problems with creativity and promotion.

    a) Whether Black folks admit it or not, the bulk of us still imitate White folks and use their definitions to explain our own world. Thus, Black creativity often is not considered creativity until White folks say it's creative.

    b) The White world is full of promoters: men and women who spend all their time looking for people, products and ideas to package, promote and sell. They do not come into the Black community for these ideas. Thus, Black creativity is disconnected from the network that turns ideas into money.

Black folks are slow on sales and almost non-existent in the field of promotion. It is difficult for Blacks to sell to other Blacks and also difficult for Blacks to sell to Whites. Those sales that *are* made by Blacks are almost always standard products rather than new creative ideas using new promotional styles. What does all this mean for the Black man or woman who wants to make money? It means there is very little competition keeping you from doing your thing once you understand the principles.

9. *FORTUNE BUILDERS GIVE UP A PIECE OF THE ACTION.*

It is very, very difficult, maybe impossible, to make a lot of money without the help of others. Black folks often destroy their own efforts at making money because they have been surrounded by so much poverty that they don't actually believe that there is enough money for their partners and suppliers to get rich with them. Blacks have been exploited for so long that they actually believe that the only way to get rich is for one person to have most of the cash at the expense of everybody else connected with the enterprise. That, my friend, is suicide.

Ray Kroc, the granddaddy of the McDonald Hamburger chain, is worth at least five hundred million dollars ($500,000,000) by selling an item that cost less than a dollar for most of the last twenty years. How did he do it? Well, one way was to help other people get rich. Today, many owners of McDonald's franchises are millionaires.

Even in something like boxing one has to think in terms of giving up a piece of the action. Nothing could be more individualistic than boxing. One man does the training, one man takes the beating and one man has to face the public regardless of the outcome. Ali made 50 million dollars over the last nineteen years; but Joe Frazier, George Foreman, Ken Norton, Don King, Herbert Muhammad, Bob Arum, Madison Square Garden and his trainer, Angelo Dundee, made millions also.

As a matter of fact, it may well be worth your while to sit down one day and turn the question completely around. Instead of asking, "How can *I* make some money?" you may need to ask, "Who can I help make a lot of money." That's what lawyers ask themselves and they come up with names like Reggie Jackson, Walt Frazier, Julius Irving, etc. etc. etc. Dig it.

10. *FORTUNE BUILDERS BUILD A TEAM.*

Not only is it difficult to make a fortune without making a lot for other people, but you would need the help of other people to go through all of the steps needed to make a fortune anyway. Everybody has a team of pros whom they consult when they are playing for the big stakes. The small fry tries to do everything himself, and usually fails at everything.

Necessary teammates would include:

1) Good Lawyer. When I was growing up a lawyer was like a doctor and dentist. They were few and far between and you hoped like hell you never needed one. Why? Because a lawyer got you out of jail or kept you from going to jail and you never wanted to be that close to jail. The idea that you would need a lawyer to help you start a business and to make money was crazy. Perry Mason never helped anybody make money and he was *the* lawyer. So goes the narrow idea of the function of the lawyer. I'd like to think the idea of what a lawyer does is much broader today but I wouldn't bet on it.

Nearly all money makers have a good lawyer. A good lawyer keeps you from making financial mistakes and structures deals for you so that you have the most advantages and the most protection. He is a teacher. He tells you what is happening, why it is happening and what the choices are. He does not say, "Leave everything to me; I'll take care of everything." He does not have such a big ego that he won't contact other attorneys if he's stuck on a point or needs some advice. He is bright and experienced, but he's hungry enough to feel that he still has to prove himself to you and everybody else to make his bundle. A good lawyer must be tested and proven over the course of time.

2) Good Real Estate Broker. Rich folks own property even when they rent apartments themselves. A good broker is one who explains the real estate game to you in a language you can understand. A good broker calls you when a hot deal comes up and explains to you why it's a good deal and gets the deal for you with as little of your own money invested in the property as possible.

3) Good Accountant. This man will eventually save you half of your yearly earnings. Why? Because that's what you will pay to the federal government in income taxes if you *don't* have one. A good accountant is an advisor who tells you how to spend your money so that most of it is yours as opposed to Uncle Sam's. He too must be a good teacher. Your goal is not to learn enough so that you won't need the accountant but to learn enough to come up with a few ideas of your own and enough to tell when he is doing a good job and when he's messing up.

4) Banking Relationships. It takes money to make money, you ever heard of that? Where do you think the money comes from . . . the banks, at least sometimes. The worse thing in the world you want to do is to go to a bank and have to go through the same motions over and over again . . . name, address, how long at your present job, etc. etc. etc. You want certain people with considerable lending authority to know you on a first name basis and you want to get free advice on how something might be financed. You want your banker *to tell you* how a deal ought to look in order for the officer or their credit committee to say, "Yes, we'll lend you the money." You also want several options to choose from so you'll need to deal with several types of banks. One kind of bank may lend on real estate, another may back a business idea while a third may approve the biggest personal line of credit of the three. You'll need different types of accounts and eventually you may even want to create a little competition so that you can get the best deal offered. It is important that the banker understand that you are a candidate for repeat business and that you are on your way to making a bundle. Banks love to help folks they think will grow wealthy.

Naturally, it will take Black folks longer to get this kind of relationship than White folks. That's why you may send your lawyer or accountant (who may or may not be White themselves) to represent you until the beginnings of an understanding are developed.

5) Other Craftsmen, Specialists and Businessmen. Whatever your thing is you are going to have to be able to reach out and contact sharp folks that can help you build or give assistance to your enterprise. Do not wait until you need them. Look for them beforehand, check their

work beforehand, check their prices beforehand and check their general reputation. With this kind of backup it is easier to take risks, easier to save money and easier to creatively use and blend the talents of other people. Remember, you are the captain of your particular ship and you will need a large crew because you're going on a hell of a trip.

11. FORTUNE BUILDERS INVEST IN PRIME REAL ESTATE.

It has been said that more men have made fortunes in real estate than all the other fortune building ideas combined. This, you see, is because the whole world is composed of pieces of real estate. There is real estate where there aren't even people. Valuable minerals, food, cloth, wood and stone are all connected to pieces of real estate.

From a Fortune Builder's point of view, investment real estate consists of one's home or homes, apartment buildings, farms, office buildings, shopping centers, graveyards, etc. etc. etc. A whole section of this book is used to discuss real estate so no long explanation is attempted here.

12. FORTUNE BUILDERS AVOID PAYING HIGH TAXES.

Black folks and liberals have attacked the income tax structure in this country for years by saying it was favoring the rich and putting an unequal burden for payment on the little man. It might seem a little odd for a Black man to advocate that his people also find means of paying less of their income in taxes. After all, it is the tax monies that pay for the many social programs that help the little man . . . right?

The facts are that the laws and rationals for income tax deductions are so incredibly confused, jumbled and vague that no one, not even I.R.S., can clearly explain or justify the system to the satisfaction of liberals or conservatives. Meanwhile, the poor and the powerless do pay more than their share in taxes and in ways that many are not even aware of. Urban people pay a higher rate of taxes and all people living in the Northeast section of this country pay a higher rate of taxes. If you happen to be Black and poor and living in a Northeastern city, you are paying through the nose in city, state and federal taxes. This has got to stop. You have got to stop paying these high taxes if you ever intend to build and keep your fortune. The first thing that Fortune Builders do is to study the income tax system to see who has to pay what, who can avoid or deduct what, and find out why and how much.

The burden of finding out these pieces of information is squarely on your own shoulders. Most people will take one look at the fine, tightly bunched print of the tax manual and throw the booklet down. "To hell if I'm going to go through all that stuff." As usual, the cost of laziness and ignorance and an uncaring attitude is high, not in just a few dollars but in thousands over time.

If you are lucky in your employment you will get a few decent raises and eventually make a good wage. At that point a more fascinating form of stupidity arises. I have actually heard with my own two ears people, Black and White, say, "I don't want anymore raises because it will put me in a higher tax bracket and it's not worth it." That, my friend, I find fascinating because this guy or girl knows that to get 20 thousand a year you must pass 15 and to get to 30 thousand you must pass 25. How in the hell can anybody say, "Don't give me money because I don't want the taxes." If the taxes worried him or her that much that they would turn down a raise, you would think that they would pick up the tax book and figure out how to save on their taxes . . . right? Wrong! Instead people will go to the bar and tell the bartender how the tax structure favors the rich. They know less about the tax system than a gym rat and refuse to learn.

The facts, brothers and sisters, is that there are over fifteen hundred ways to deduct expenses from your income and thereby reduce the final amount of money that you pay taxes on. Any good book store will have at least three or more books that explain how to do this in a simple step-by-step way. You don't have to read the whole tax guide. But you will not find these books in the sex novel section of the bookstore; you will have to walk all the way over to the other side and look under the business and finance section.

The tax laws do not necessarily favor the rich as they do the self-employed and property owners. And one can be far from rich and own real estate and some sort of part or full time business. At some point you will be able to dump this whole task into the hands of your accountant. If you really begin to do well, your accountant can help you in *tax planning*. You see, rich folks don't wait until April 15 to find out how much they *owe*. They start from January 1 of each year to plan their expenses, investments and deductions to *make sure* that they won't owe much, if anything, when April 15 of the *following year* rolls around. As a matter of fact, some rich folks have been known to scramble around in September looking to *spend* twenty-five thousand dollars on a business that has *lost* fifty thousand dollars or more in order to keep from paying high taxes. Now that sounds crazy to *you*, doesn't it? There is a whole lot to this game and it's never too early to start learning. This is especially true if you are Black.

13. *FORTUNE BUILDERS KEEP RECORDS.*

Records can make and save you money, did you know that? Records tell you how you are spending your time and your (or somebody else's) money. How else can you make money except by spending your time and money wisely? In business there is usually some part of the general sales that is making a great deal of money while other parts are only breaking even or worse. You will not know which is which if you do not keep records. You may have thought that the hamburger giants got rich selling hamburgers, didn't you? Wrong! They got rich selling *french fries.* Compare the cost of raising potatoes with raising cattle. Compare the cost of slicing potatoes with getting hamburger from a cow. Then check to see how much you are being charged for a half of a potato versus a half a pound of beef. It shouldn't take you long to see where most of the profit lies. Next time that cute waitress asks you if you would like to have fries with your hamburger, you'll know why.

You can only make record profits if you have the records to show the profit. Speaking of records, how many records do rock stars actually sell? Would it surprise you to know that many a Black performer has sold a half million or so records and got paid for only half that amount? That's another way of saying that Black folks better start concentrating on keeping records of just more than their records.

Records are important for basically three reasons:
1) They tell you where you stand, what you have to buy, sell, reorder, liquidate and keep. They tell you when to take on new people and when to let some go.
2) Records are needed for all tax matters. They tell you what expenses you can deduct, and they will be absolutely necessary of the I.R.S. wants to audit (checkup on) you.
3) Banks want to see your records before they give you the time of day. Banks want to see the profit and loss records or you'll get nothing but a wish of good luck.

14. *FORTUNE BUILDERS GIVE EXTREME VALUE TO THEIR TIME.*

Have you ever seen an executive, a leader, doctor, lawyer or any other professional who didn't have an appointment book? Probably not. This is because Fortune Builders do not take each day as it comes; they plan what they are going to do. Sometimes they plan what they have to do for each hour of each working day. They do not trust their memories (regardless of their brillance) to remember every detail; *they write it down!* The time is budgeted like money. Black folks in particular find a whole range of problems crop up when they begin to try to budget their time. Let's look at a typical situation:

A local Black person wins an important position, but his "home boys" and family don't understand why they can't just drop by and talk like they use to. They are often very angered when they hear that they have to go through the secretary to get an appointment to see their old friend. They may accuse him or her of "acting sidity or bourgeois." This is because Black folks do not, on the whole, understand that time is money. The idea that time is money is rarely seen in the job orientation that most of us experience.

There is a common expression in the Black community called "C.P. time." C.P. time means Colored People Time and is used to express the idea that Black folks will most likely be late to some significant degree for an agreed deadline or appointment. Usually there is no harm in the lateness and both parties usually automatically account for such differences and it becomes part of the overall planning. To be late for something in the Black community will rarely ever cost anyone money or financial penalty. Thus, the connection between time and money is seldom made.

Fortune Builders on the other hand are self-employed which means if they don't do something with their time they don't get any money. A Fortune Builder often lives in a world of pressures and deadlines. He or she can actually do their thing correctly and economically; but if they miss an appointment here, a payment there and deliver the merchandise at something other than the agreed time, they have to pay. Their loss of customers and orders bites into their income.

Secretaries are a very important factor in time use also. Have you ever seen a rich person without a secretary? A secretary is an organizer of your time and a saver of time. He/she is also a cushion between you and the bullshit of the outside world. You know, I assume that there is much more bullshit in the world than there is serious business. Successful Fortune Builders find this out in the early days of their company. As soon as they got a little reputation of success, as soon as people began to think they might have a little money, all the neighborhood bullshit came running to their door. Usually it was all harmless but it ate up time. So you sit a secretary by the door, and it is his or her job to come to work everyday with his or her shoulder pads and hold off the bullshit like a Pittsburg Steeler lineman.

15. *FORTUNE BUILDERS OWN THEIR BUSINESS.*

It has been written that 98% of all people who earn $50,000 a year or more do so in their own business. That means that only 2% earn this sum as salary at some type of job. This statistic is for White folks. I would say that the figure might be something like 99.8% of all Black folks earning this kind of money do it by doing their own thing. Why do I say that? Simple. A person making 50K per year is an executive at a top management level in most companies in the nation. We know that among the corporate leaders there are few Black faces.

In the government structure, few big city mayors make more than

50K. Fewer Black mayors make 50K. And very, very few city employees make more than their mayors. In the federal government 50K is a GS rating in the stars as far as Black folks are concerned. Many of those who do make it are in appointed positions lasting four to a maximum of maybe eight years. Then they have to scuffle all over again.

Professional practices count as small business in the broad sense of the word. Doctors, a few lawyers and others make a sizable portion of the Blacks over the 50K category. Obviously, Black pro athletes are those rare persons way over 50K who do not run their own business. Just as obvious is their limited numbers.

16. *FORTUNE BUILDERS HAVE MORE THAN ONE THING GOING ON AT THE SAME TIME.*

It is difficult for anybody, especially Black folks, to make really big money (say over 100K per year) doing just one thing. Therefore, Fortune Builders, by design, seek additional avenues to express their creativity and to make bigger money. Success breeds more success because once a person learns the basics of any business, well he or she can do well in related business. This is especially true if you can use some of your same customers to support both businesses (remember Gladys and her record store-liquor store business). This is called *diversification.*

A second reason Fortune Builders get involved in other enterprises is because whereas they might not want to cash in on their success, *somebody else* might. This is especially true if our Fortune Builder has a well-known name. Bill Cosby, for example, advertises everything it seems. Does he have to run all over the country telling jokes to strangers at one o'clock in the morning? Not if he doesn't want to. Other people want to pay him for his success. The stories about athletes getting 500K from their sport and two to three times that doing other odds and ends are common.

Finally, the third reason Fortune Builders have more than one enterprise going at once is for security reasons. Any business or enterprise can fall on hard times. The stock market, the auto industry and housing development are three giant areas of commerce where people have been wiped out because they had all their eggs in one basket. The wise Fortune Builder can rest a little easier if he or she knows that they are being fed by more than one source of income.

17. *FORTUNE BUILDERS SAVE SOME OF THEIR MONEY AND LIVE BELOW THEIR MEANS.*

How can one be so sure that Fortune Builders live below their means? The answer is very simple. They invest a portion of their money. One cannot invest in anything if he or she does not have a portion of their income left over to invest. The number one investment is usually one's own business enterprise. Everyone, including White folks, has difficulty borrowing money on an untried idea. People understand how competitive the business world is and how easy it is to have high hopes and dreams and have an enterprise fall flat on its face. For this reason it is almost always a requirement for a person to put his money where his mouth is. Many, many a person has taken the income that they could have used for a thousand enjoyable uses for themselves and their families and put it away in savings towards starting a business. Often this habit of saving and reinvesting profits back into a business lasts long after the doors of the business has opened. The reasons for having savings even multiply. There may be a bad year in sales, a new unexpected expense or business could boom and you need to buy more equipment or products.

A statement was made earlier that going after wealth and business can destroy a marriage. The idea most folks have is that the dissatisfied mate cannot make the adjustment of the Fortune Builder being away from home so much, and this is true. Just as deadly, however, is for the dissatisfied mate to see that *the business, not the family,* is getting the greater part of the cash profits. The family goes on scrimping so that the business will survive. Thus, many unhappy mates tell their partner where they can shove the business and leave. In the Black community this reality is probably a lot more prevalent than in the White. The Black businessman probably had less savings to begin with and entered a borderline business and/or a borderline neighborhood. The atmosphere toward Black business is negative from the standpoint of White financial support, police protection, insurance protection and young criminal offenders. The pressure in the home to pull out and stop "throwing good money after bad" is often great and decisions have to be made.

In any event, Fortune Builders in the early years learn how to put the money away so that these money seeds will grow into redwood trees in the near future.

18.   *FORTUNE BUILDERS KNOW HOW TO SHOP.*

It really doesn't make sense to bust your butt working hard and earning good money if you are just going to go out and pay all the ridiculously high prices that many retail outlets charge for their merchandise. Rich folks learn to pay wholesale or reduced prices on virtually everything. The new science of bargain shopping is told in many books available on the market today. One can buy houses and cars at great savings through estate sales and bankruptcy auctions. There are outlet manufacturers selling furniture, clothes and almost any other item you can think of at greatly reduced prices.

Black folks often complain that the businesses in their community are White owned and the profits are taken out of their community and go to the suburbs. This is a fact. It is a less important fact than the fact that Black folks pay absolutely insane prices for the food, clothing and furniture in these "community stores." Black folks are not paying merely for food, clothing and furniture when they buy in their community. They are paying for the high real estate taxes the owner is paying, the high insurance costs, the high vandalism and theft of merchandise costs, the high percentage of bad-paying credit customers, advertising costs and other pass-on costs.

Shopping malls are another extremely expensive place to shop. Why? Because when you shop at a mall you pay for acres and acres of parking lot space. You pay for the fantastic energy bills that run the lights, the "climate controls" and the other electrical fixtures. You pay the service charge for the major credit cards whether you use the credit cards or not. You pay the heavy advertising costs that makes your Sunday paper twice the size of any other issue. A host of other "pass along" charges are added to the prices of most products in the malls.

Where should Black folks buy if not the neighborhood stores or the mall? The warehouses and outlet shops in the larger cities near you, that's where. The factory areas where the air smells bad, the streets are full of dirt and pot holes and the merchandise is piled all on top of each other. That's where you go. There will be no bags, no cute salesgirls, no returns, no fitting rooms, no lights or music playing . . . just bargains. Fun shopping, convenience shopping and bargain shopping are three distinct things. It's cool to do them all as long as you know which is which.

19. FORTUNE BUILDERS HAVE GOOD CREDIT, BORROW HEAVILY AND USE OTHER PEOPLE'S MONEY.

It is almost impossible to make a fortune in this country without borrowing money. The idea you see, the main idea of making a fortune in the first place is to borrow as much money as you can. Say you put a million of somebody else's money to work in a business. You work that enterprise so that it makes twenty percent gross profit or $200,000. From those profits you pay half or so in bills and payments toward repaying the million dollar debt. You walk away with 100 thousand which came as the result of your time and brains and somebody else's money.

Now before someone lends you a million dollars, somebody is going to have to lend you a hundred dollars or something valued at a hundred dollars. If you make your payments on time, they may lend you more than a hundred K the next time. Miss your payments or stop payments and a little bad mark goes by your name at a central credit bureau serving your metropolitan area. You see our grade school teachers lied to us. They told us that our report card would follow us around wherever we would go. The truth is that nobody gives a damn about your report card.

But almost every kind of store or firm lending money pays money every month to look at your *credit report card*. Many people think they have gotten away with something when they duck creditors and keep merchandise. Black folks especially feel a sense of pride in out-foxing the old bastards downtown who have been ripping them off for years. The problem usually comes back to haunt them later and the value of whatever they "bought" will never equal the loss of their credit standing. Some come to their senses and get it straightened out eventually. Others rationalize that they'll just pay cash for whatever they need and to hell with credit. As long as they never try to buy anything over a few hundred dollars they may be in good shape. The kinds of things that Fortune Builders want and buy cost a little more than a few hundred dollars.

20. *FORTUNE BUILDERS TAKE ADVANTAGE OF OTHER PEOPLE'S MISFORTUNE*

There is great tendency to confuse the idea of taking *advantage* of people's misfortune and taking an *unfair advantage* of other people's misfortune. The key word is *unfair* and therein lies all the meaning in the world. Let us look at a couple of illustrations.

Leaping Louie leaped high to block a shot in a practice basketball game and came down on the wrong part of his foot. Leaping Louie became Limping Louie as his foot was placed in a cast for 16 weeks. Redi Teddy was inserted into the starting lineup and averaged thirty points a game for the Los Angeles Lakers. By the end of the season, Louie had his cast off and the coach was stuck with the usual decision. Do you put Louie back in the starting lineup simply because he was in the lineup before the injury? Or do you stick with a ballplayer that's been averaging 30 points a game for four months? That question doesn't concern us. Our question is did Teddy take advantage of Louie's problem? Yes. Did he take *unfair* advantage of Louie's problem? No, because somebody had to replace Louie. The team had to go on playing and if it wasn't Teddy, it would have been someone else. The team and the public and Teddy are all quite happy that a new star was born. Even Leaping Louie was glad that the team continued its winning ways in his absence. This situation happens all the time in sports, the movie industry and everywhere when the star is not available.

Now most of us are not stars nor are we waiting in the wings to replace or become stars. Still, there ought to be situations in society for us to take advantage of people's misfortune. Let's look at this example:

Fred, a balding banker, had been turned down for his last four requests for promotion after twenty years of dedicated service to the bank. Angered and feeling betrayed, he siphons about 50 thousand out of the bank's deposits and tries to spend his way to a sense of fulfillment. The president learns of the theft and tells Fred the following: "Fred, you've been a loyal, valuable employee for 20 years. For that reason we are not going to press charges against you if you repay us in one week after which time you will have sixty days to look for other employment." Fred has one asset, his house, worth 150K with a mortgage balance of 30K. He goes to a realtor and tells him to sell the house quick; he must have the cash in one week. The realtor calls you because you have cash and because he knows he can't find a lawyer, get bank financing and schedule a closing in less than a week's time. Fred's mortgage company says they must be paid off if the property is going to change hands. You have 100K (tops) and that's what you offer Fred for his house. He takes it. The bank gets their 30K and Fred gets 70K of which 50K goes to the bank he stole from. Fred has 20K on which to make a new start in life and you have a 150K house which cost you 100K. This is a gain in value of 50K in less than a week. Did you take unfair advantage of Fred? Hell no, you were more like a fire engine coming to put out a raging fire in record time. You saved Fred from jail, gave him a nest egg to start a new life and paid off his biggest debt all in less time than it would take for the world's richest institutions to move a muscle.

Building a fortune fast is very often dependant on how well, how fast and how quietly you can move to help someone whose luck has fallen due to no ill will or deed on the part of anyone in particular. They usually need cash fast. The amount or the speed or the item which they are giving in return for the cash often narrows the field of potential helpers down to a very few. When people have little choice they take what they can get. The world pays a high price to problem solvers and a higher price to quick problem solvers. Why can't that person be you?

21. FORTUNE BUILDERS MAKE EXTENSIVE USE OF THE MEDIA.

The media in the United States of America is simply phenomenal. It includes hundreds of television stations, thousands of radio stations, and tens of thousands of printed publications. What this media has done is create a mass culture whereby over two hundred million people stretched out thousands of miles apart live extremely similar lifestyles and have extremely similar tastes. I don't know how many miles lie between Seattle, Washington and Miami Florida, but let us assume it is four thousand. You can search all over the world and you probably are not very likely to find two people or two families living four thousand miles apart with so much similarity in language, customs, beliefs, goals and day-to-day living habits. This is no accident. The media programs all of us into liking, believing and buying the same things. The number one record in New York is bound to be within the top five in Los Angeles. If the style is mini skirts in San Diego you can bet they are wearing them in New Hampshire also. The common man in the street has no real impact on what goes on television or the other media because he or she is not the programmer. The common man in the street is the programmee, the one to be programmed. I think everyone has realized at one time or another that almost anything can be sold to the gullible public if it is repeated enough times for their ears and eyes to notice. Have you ever caught yourself singing a record or commercial that you didn't even like? You probably have and the reason was simple. The message was simple, even silly or ridiculous, and it is banged into your head everyday, three, four or more times a day. America is a name brand, fashion designer economy and the names come to you through magazines and newspaper advertisements as well as the tube. This means that Fortune Builders, who sooner or later have to sell a lot of something, need their names or their products' names out in public competing for your attention and dollars. The philosophy is simply make a thousand aware so that fifty will buy; let a million see so that 5%, 50,000, will buy. If you sell fifty thousand of anything you will begin to make a lot of money.

Black businesses which mostly cater to small communities often do not bother to advertise believing "the word will get around." The problem often lies not in the fact that they would do better spending the money on advertising but in the fact that their business is designed to be small. It makes large scale advertising rather pointless. Who ever heard of a nationally known barbershop?

Fortune Builders may eventually put themselves in the media so you may eventually see their face. This widespread public exposure creates a positive image and people begin to see you as having more power and influence than you really do. They treat you with added respect and deference when they meet you "in person." The power of being a "media star" is impressive in financial circles; and doors, always closed before, now open up. Everybody likes to know or be associated with someone "famous" no matter what the person's claim to fame is. A famous beer commercial actor can draw just as many autograph seekers as a sports star, given the right circumstances.

Obviously, it is much harder for a Black person to gain media coverage because of our extreme lack of control in the media. Those media that we do control unfortunately choose to push crime stories and sob stories in our face every week while giving poor attention to the positive things going on in the communities. The only answer is to pay for your own media and associate yourself with as many progressive groups as possible. Everyone that you might possibly come in contact with must know what you do for a living. Don't you think the world's most widely known shoeshiner is probably also the richest?

22. FORTUNE BUILDERS DELEGATE NON-ESSENTIAL TASKS TO OTHERS.

There are three groups of people that Fortune Builders need in building their fortune. First are their team members such as lawyers, bankers, etc. The second group are his business partners; people who he has given a piece of the action to (a percentage of the business profits). The third group is composed of the functionaires: the employees. These people do what they are told to do for a salary in order for the Fortune Builder to do *his* work better, faster, easier or cheaper. Too often Black businesspersons try to do everything themselves and eventually put just as much time to answering phones as they do going after financing or new product lines. Obviously, in the beginning all Fortune Builders do at least most things themselves. But as their time grows limited and more important, they move to do only the important things. Building a good support staff is the key to turning over lesser important tasks to others. One has to look just as hard, maybe harder, for a good receptionist, secretary and assistant as one does for a good attorney.

23. FORTUNE BUILDERS HAVE MADE A SUBSTANTIAL COMMITMENT OF FIVE TO TEN OR MORE YEARS TO THEIR ENTERPRISE.

America is an impatient nation and speed seems to be a desirable goal of everything. We gladly give up the opportunity for good food if we can have fast food. Certainly fast fortunes are more desirable than gradual fortunes. There are many stories of bright ambitious folks who have made a fortune overnight. Almost all were White and usually some fortune combination of timing, connections, luck, backing, etc., happened to have come together under a specific set of circumstances which made for an explosion of wealth. In most instances, however, you will find the Fortune Builder, no matter how lucky or bright, has been pushing his thing for a number of years—at least five and probably closer to ten. This sustained period of effort is a great key to success. Failures foster learning and victories trigger encouragement and energy in quick succession. Most realistic wealth builders understand that time and phases are a part of all building processes and thus plan for the long haul. It is easier to be persistent if the mind is already prepared to undergo years of preparation and struggle.

In the Black community it must be remembered that our rich young musicians and athletes are professionals with ten or fifteen years experience even at twenty-two years old. They have put their time in on virtually a day in-day out basis year after year. Everybody has to pay some kind of dues, and if you understand how much you have to pay at the outset, it should make it easier to go through the process. It is also very important to understand that there is a very big difference between going through struggle simply because you're poor in the ghetto and going through struggle to put forth a particular idea or concept. You do not get credit in this life simply for absorbing pain. You have to focus on the goal for the required period of time *in spite of the pain*. The pain, the poverty, the lack of support are the results of being Black and exploited in this country and do not count for anything other than making you stronger *after* you succeed in your thing. But fail to succeed and you're just another casualty of American historical circumstances whose wretched life will not mean anything to anybody and who will be forgotten shortly after you leave this planet. If that sounds harsh, it's because that's how harsh reality can be.

24. *FORTUNE BUILDERS EITHER HAVE A SUPPORTIVE SPOUSE OR NO SPOUSE AT ALL.*

Other than attitude, one's spouse is probably the next most important single factor in one's life which will determine their success in fortune building. Any marriage counselor will tell you that the lack of money or money problems are a great cause in marital problems, arguments and breakups. I would suspect that this is even much more so in the Black community. It would be nice to think that strong determination to lick poverty would have a resulting positive benefit to marriages, but such is just not the case. Making money, especially against the hardships that Black folks face, is an *intense* enterprise. It requires concentration of physical effort, mental energy, free-flowing imaginative thoughts, discipline, saving, etc. A single person can resign themselves to a hard work, programmed lifestyle much easier than making the collective decision for mates, children and extended family members who do not understand or agree with the purpose or outcome. This creates a crisis for all Fortune Builders. Thousands, maybe millions, of marriages have gone by the board as a consequence. I think it is a tragedy for Black marriages to fail on this point since poverty and lack of freedom and opportunity is so clearly our predicament. Why lose the unity while struggling toward the goal. It's even more tragic that our ancestors wanted so much to have the opportunities that we hesitate to milk. Certainly, we wouldn't have to work as hard as they, and there would be so much more to show for it. Finally, the best part of all would be the knowledge that

Black kids would be exposed to strong parental figures and would not have to struggle as much themselves if they choose not to. If you feel your mate cannot understand these kinds of ideas when they are so clear to you, then you must seriously question the compatability of your relationship.

We have come to the end of this chapter, and I hope it has proven valuable. The major purpose of this chapter was the defining of the key factors that the rich use to make and hold on to their money. Even more important for Black readers, however, is the realization that racism should not keep you from performing any of these twenty-four steps. This is not to say that race will not be a factor. It will be. But race is not a *paralyzing* factor that would make action impossible.

Now that we have approached the problem (gaining wealth) from one vantage point, namely studying the success model, let us approach it from another. We need to study the failure model. There is much to be learned by viewing both sides. None of us are either total successes nor total failures. Only by discovering our strengths and weaknesses and by looking at both sides of the coin can we determine where we are and how far we have to go.

What's Holding Black Folks in Poverty

Our study of making money will be approached from a different point of view in this chapter. I think that you, the reader, will get a comprehensive understanding of how to improve your economic condition not only by applying the principles of the rich but also by studying yourself to see what you must *not* do.

The conditions that hold Black folks in poverty are both internal and external in nature. For the purposes of this book, I will define internal as being those factors over which you have substantial control. These factors would include your education, your energy, creative ability, contacts, job skills, choice of mate, number of children, etc.

The external factors are those over which you have very little or no control and would include racism, the interest rates, natural disasters, etc. Of all the factors and variables that have been at work on Black folks in the last say 100 years influencing our ability to survive or perish, one has stood out among the rest: racism. Racism is continuous and unyielding. Black folks can eventually adjust to the price of oil, natural disaster, fire and the loss of a job. But racism is like a shadow following you constantly everywhere you go, or so it seems. I think it is beneficial in this volume to look at reality straight in the eye and realize the following:

a. Racism (the belief of Whites that they are better, more intelligent or more deserving of some privilege or opportunity for no other reason than the fact that they are White) is a reality in all White folks for one reason or another and to some degree or another. But racism doesn't stop all White folks from working in partnership with non-Whites (Blacks included) when there is a buck to be made. This is proven every day.

b. Racism has been used by many of us Blacks as an excuse for lack of determination in pursuing our goal simply because it was a pain in the ass and dampened our spirits. Every single successful Black person in the history of this country, whether they were rich or not, had to overcome racism. It is probably less of an excuse for failing now, for the strong and the determined, than ever before in the history of this racist nation.

c. You can control, if you decide to, so many factors in your life and you can learn to analyze so many situations in your life that you can actually force White folks (at least the ones you "need" and the ones who "need" you) to change the way that they respond to you and "get over." Gil Scott Heron has said, "It ain't no such thing as a Superman." I agree. But when you understand how Muhammad Ali, Wilt Chamberlain, Paul Robeson, Don King and Dr. Martin Luther King "forced" White folks to change the way they responded and reacted to them, then you understand what I mean by overcoming racism. I do not mean that you must be a "great" man or woman to change the face of racism. But once you are serious about yourself and your goals, say what you mean and mean what you say, and force all parties to respect you and what you stand for, you will find certain White folks ready to do business. They may be racist, but most of them ain't crazy.

I will not dwell too much more on racism in this book because I believe that positive-minded persons should concentrate on doing all the correct and positive things and the negative things, like racism, will be much less of a factor. Action on your part, not my discussion in this book, will expose the shortcomings of the so-called all powerful deterent of racism.

The factors holding Black folks in poverty are for the most part not racially identifiable. Most of the things that hold us in poverty are the same things that hold poor White folks in poverty. The faster individuals from either group overcome their drawbacks, the faster they'll close in on the pot of gold. As you may have gathered from all the discussion above, I will list only the internal factors in this chapter. It makes no sense to list things to be worked on if you don't have any control over them in the first place. You will learn later, however, that there is tremendous money in solving even the so-called insolvable or "terrible" problems.

The following is a partial list of those habits, problems or situations which hold Black folks in poverty. They are not necessarily in any particular order, but I would be inclined to comment more on what I believe to be the most important ones unless, of course, the point is so obvious that it doesn't need much in the way of elaboration or explanation.

1. LACK OF AWARENESS OF WEALTH BUILDING PRINCIPLES.

I think that it is pretty obvious that more Black folks would have escaped poverty if they understood in a concrete way the principles of how money is made in this country. We have reviewed them in the previous chapter. In a sense this factor, numbered 1, could really be the failure to apply the twenty-four factors mentioned earlier. Thus, I could say that Black folks are poor because they don't have a vision, use time or media, have a team, invest in real estate, etc. White folks probably got their knowledge from their parents, their environment and practical experience. I'm not sure if the educational system served them any better than anyone else as far as the knowledge of making money is concerned. Even business courses probably gained meaning simply because there were practical experiences within which to reflect the "book information." Obviously, Black folks didn't have much, if any, of these tools to work from.

2. A "GOOD" JOB.

I know it sounds strange to say that a "good" job keeps Black folks in poverty (or at least away from wealth), but I can think of nothing more dangerous to the ambitious, talented Black person than a good job. To be black and have a good job *usually* means that the following took place or is taking place:

a) You went to college.

b) You competed against Whites and/or other Blacks for the job and won out.

c) You have responsibility which you are proud of.

d) You have an image, a social, professional and intellectual image which gives you your understanding of your own self worth. In a sense you have become your job.

e) Finally, the two last nails in the coffin called "the good job" are the promise of future advancement and the promise of security (benefits, pension, stuff like that).

What I've tried to point out above is a person who is now pretty much out of control of his life. He or she is a "company man or woman." The company holds out promises which all Blacks realize are vague and usually renegged upon, yet we give the company our life in exchange for whatever it is prepared to give in return. The higher we rise up the corporate ladder, the more out of control we are. The more cautious we become in speech, dress, mannerisms, values and the list goes on. We move our home when the company says move. Now for this "good job" person to risk his salary, his social-professional image and standing, his benefits and "security" and his dream of an assistant vice presidency to strike out on his own is absolutely inconceivable. If you try to explain that there is more freedom (and a hundred thousand dollars) in operating his own McDonalds than there is in playing invisible zombie at corporate headquarters for a thirty thousand dollar "executive position," it doesn't register. He's been in the company for fifteen years doing what he (or she) was told. Freedom, real money, ownership of the assets, these ideas simply do not sink in. In a real sense a Black with a "good job" in a corporation he's worked for for ten years is very much like a convict who has been in prison for ten years or more. Neither one of them can make it on "the outside" regardless of how much strength and character they demonstrate "inside."

3. FEAR OF FAILURE (THAT "WHAT WILL THEY SAY SYNDROME).

Many, many people, especially Blacks, would have and could have done some fantastic things in their lives if only they weren't scared of failing. I don't know how anyone could ever adopt the attitude that "I will only try to do this new challenge if I can know ahead of time that I will be perfect." Doesn't that sound stupid? Yet, that is apparently what many people expect.

Actually, I believe fear of failure is not the exact term. It's more like the fear of "what will they say if I mess up?" People sometimes care too much about their image. Young men go off to war to kill or be killed rather than be called a coward because that would hurt "their image." People fear failure not because *they* couldn't deal with it but because they would have a lot of emotional problems if ridiculed by "friends" or family.

Many times the friends and family will have a fear of failure for you. If you tell them that you think you would like to try "such and such," they may immediately give you 118 reasons why you shouldn't do it or try it. Most mean well. They actually believe that they are protecting you from the "certain" failure and disappointment that they believe is sure to follow. If you are wishy-washy, you're easily convinced to give up something that you didn't even try.

Most people will always *say,* "I don't care what anybody thinks of me" and yet be very controlled by what other people think of them.

Money hungry go-getters say it and mean it, and only after they have the wealth that they were after do they start to really care what other people care about them.

I think Black folks are extremely affected by this problem because:

a) Segregated society forces us to live together and so it is more important, in a sense, to protect one's image in a community from which one knows he cannot escape very easily.

b) Black folks are so quick, so hard and so vicious in the ridicule that they give each other that the emotions get inflamed to a greater degree than the situation merits many, many times. Thus, extra precaution is used to avoid nasty confrontations over silly situations.

4. *NEW LUXURY CARS (PAYMENTS)*.

When I was real small I used to hear Black folks say, "White folks are racist; they think all a Black wants is a Cadillac." Well I have lived in Black communities on both coasts and I am not a White racist. But it almost appears to me that all Black folks want is a Cadillac (or a Mark V or a Mercedes). The stories about Black folks and big cars are many, long and at this point probably boring. But I think we do need to review some facts.

    a) Luxury cars lose tremendous value in their first two years of use. People have sought to resell their big cars six months after it leaves the showroom and get quoted offers of four thousand or more dollars less than what they paid for the car.

    b) Big cars cost more to run, maintain, insure, repair and clean. It eats into your pocket several ways at the same time.

    c) New big cars are habit forming. You may buy a new big luxury car and take three to four years to pay for it. As soon as the car is paid for (but usually before), you say to yourself, "Well it's time for me to get a new ride. I worked hard; I owe it to myself," and put yourself in the hole for another three years or so. You eventually have a permanent bill which keeps you from gaining other credit, purchasing a decent house for your family and saving any money. With no other credit, savings or home, you stay in poverty, Mark V and all.

Maybe numbers will show a clearer picture:

Example A

A $12,000 car paid over 4 years is a monthly note of about $250. You pay $250 per month rent. Your total payment for these 2 debts is $500 a month.

At the end of 4 years you have a $12,000 car now worth about $4,000. You also have your same old apartment.

Compare $4,000 in value to $14,000. There is more than a 300% difference.

Example B

A cheaper used compact car costs you $3,500. The monthly rate is $100. Because of the lower monthly car payment you qualify for a mortgage to buy a house. The house costs 25K and the monthly payment including taxes is $300. Each month you use about $100 to do general repairs and improvements in the house. Your total expenses for car and housing is also $500 per month.

At the end of four years you own an older compact car worth $1,000. You also own a house now worth about 35K, but you only owe 22K because of the payments you have made the last 4 years.

Your total assets are worth about 14 thouand dollars to you now.

5. *TELEVISION.*

Television is deadly. Its value to Black folks especially is less than zero in most cases. Fortune Builders are active; television makes you passive. Fortune Builders deal with reality; television makes you believe in fantasy. Fortune Builders learn to admire themselves; television watchers admire the people on television. Fortune Builders love their work; television watchers work to buy a television they love. I could go on all day, but I think you see the point.

Television doesn't add in any way to the value of a person's intellect, skill, morality, intuition or much of anything else. It *does* teach you how things are sold. National statistics say we stare at this tube about five hours a night every night. That's thirty-five hours a week or four working days. Do you know how much money can be made in four working days? If you feel you must watch television, at least get paid for it. This country has thousands of security jobs, bartender jobs, gas station and waitress jobs where the tube is going all the time. Thirty-five hours times four dollars an hour is one hundred and forty dollars. If you can make a hundred and forty dollars a week (extra) watching television, go do it until you learn better.

6. *SEXUAL ESCAPADES.*

Black folks generally live in the oldest, uggliest, dirtiest parts of town. We are given the lowest paid jobs and the kinds of jobs that few people like to do and few feel a sense of pride in doing well. As human beings and observers of the general life in America, we know that we are being shortchanged. Individually and collectively we strain to put some color, joy and excitement in our life. Because of our low income it must be *low cost* color, *low cost* joy and *low cost* excitement. The consistent winner is sexual conquest. It is a troubled person who doesn't find sex colorful, joyful and exciting.

In the Black community there is a lot of sexual activity going on for a whole host of reasons, including those stated above. Unfortunately, sex, like anything and everything else, can be over done and can imprison the excessive participants in a web of poverty. I think I need to explain this. How can too much sex lead to poverty?

For a poor person to escape poverty he has to compensate for the low value of his unskilled work time by putting in more time to net a livable wage. This means he has to work longer hours. It takes discipline and sacrifice to work extra hours day after day, month after month. It is only natural for any man or woman to want to "hang out" and be with the opposite sex. If you have to constantly restrain yourself from pleasurable sexual experience and trade unattractive low-paying work in its place, it can be a tremendous strain. Many people cannot fight their urges, attractions and propositions and so they spend a great deal of time in bed in the early evenings.

Once this tendency gets addictive, our would-be Fortune Builders lose the use of his biggest asset: his or her time. In a young man's life this may not be such a big thing and the lost opportunity can perhaps be made up for at a later date. But when an aging man in the prime of life—late thirties, forties and early fifties—is still chasing skirts with a full family at home to provide for, he can generally be written off. For women who spend a lot of time in the bedroom, the consequences can be worse. Unwanted children or abortions, guilt complexes and frustration at not "capturing" a permanent "main man" can set in the kinds of attitudes and self-concepts that makes winning the money game virtually impossible. I hope you dig what I mean.

7. *DRUGS AND ALCOHOL.*

Drugs and alcohol are heavies, real big heavies. I won't pretend for one fraction of a second that I know the answer to these trips. There are many, many causes of drug and alcohol addiction, and I believe that one of the biggest is hopelessness. Thousands of people, Black and White, believe that the only control they have over their life is when they are high simply because they are out of everybody *else's* control. I believe three things about addressing the needs of the addict:

    a) Those that are not too far gone or have very strong character can eventually muster the willpower to kick the habit if they want to.

    b) One of the few reasons that a junkie may ever even want to break his habit is when he learns that there might be a possibility that he or she can regain substantial control and power over their own life and environment.

    c) That the ability to earn one's own way in the world is the key to regaining this power and control over one's life and environment. In other words, a junkie has to see it is possible not only for him or her to clean up, but live a good life after cleaning up. Otherwise, what is it all for? This means they have to learn the ability to make a good income, and I believe that any drug program that does not address this question has to be missing something.

8. *PRISON RECORDS.*

There are countless studies which exist on the U.S. prison system, and they all say pretty much the same thing:

    a) Minorities are jailed at a much higher proportion than their numbers in the general population.

b) Minorities receive longer sentences for the same type of crimes that Whites commit.
c) Prison systems do not rehabilitate but simply punish.
d) Prison systems do not equip inmates with marketable skills during the imprisonment period.

Black folks suffer tremendous emotional, economic, spiritual and physical damage at the hands of the American prison system. My own thinking on the plight of the released inmate is that his fate is very much related to his attitude about himself and life. What I mean is that if every released inmate wanted to cry the blues, feel sorry for him or herself and rationalize the futility of putting forth the extra effort necessary to get over, all the excuses are available to him. He can constantly dwell on his past and his losses and soon find himself striking out in anger at the world and possibly find him or herself right back in the slam.

If, on the other hand, our former offenders can get their heads to-gether and realize that they still can gain wealth, comfort and security in spite of their past, then the possibilities are endless. A prison record can be a handicap in acquiring a top job. But since we now understand that a top job is not only unnecessary *but actually gets in the way of gaining wealth,* that lost job opportunity shouldn't bother them. A prison record doesn't prevent you from educating yourself, saving and investing your money, owning property or any of the other factors relating to gaining wealth. It may take a little longer and require going through a few more changes, but I think the results will be worth it for you and your family. What is needed is a solid plan, right? Read on!

9. *UNEMPLOYMENT.*

Black unemployment has been cited as the number one cause for Black poverty, and you'll find no argument here on that fundamental point. What I'd like to do here, however, is to make a few comments which may change the way you look at unemployment and the unem-ployed.

Many jobs go unfilled in this country not because the requirements are beyond the capacity of Black folks, but because of the job's low pay and prestige. Most people look at a job as an end in itself rather than a means to greater ends. Because so much status, value and self-concept is tied to what a person does for a living, many people would rather collect unemployment or welfare than work on a job which they believe degrades them. Up to this point this attitude is rather understandable. But the Action Plan presented further on in this book may alter your thinking on this point.

How would you feel if I told you that there is an occupation in this country which doesn't require a college education, which could lead to a lot of money and, best of all, from which you could never really get fired? Would that excite you? Well, get ready. *It's Sales!* That's right, sales. Think about it for a moment. If you could learn to sell, learn to enjoy selling and profit from selling, you would never be out of work as long as you lived in the United States of America. This is because America is one big supermarket where everything is always for sale. The easiest thing in the world to do is to pick up a paper and find a sales job. Millions of people in this country make their living selling things. Only a small part of this number is composed of Black folks. Many Blacks who do sell for a living do so on a salary basis rather than a commission basis. There are many reasons for this feeble representation of Blacks in sales, and it will be discussed in a future chapter. For right now I think it is enough to say that Black folks will never get their fair share of jobs in this country as long as they continue to shy away from the number one job in America—the job of selling.

10. *ISOLATION IN THE NEGATIVE ENVIRONMENT OF THE GHETTO.*

There would be many more success stories from the Black community if the many energetic, talented individuals were not so isolated in pockets of negativity and helplessness. While it is true that only the strong and the determined will survive, there are many situations which would test the will and sanity of the strongest among us. Poor home life and school systems can ruin many a talented youngster and leave them as prime candidates to absorb the distractions of drugs, crime, alcohol or other unproductive enterprises. A vicious cycle is created whereby Black folks are drawn into the underlife of the community thereby increasing its numbers and attracting even more recruits.

11. *POOR BUSINESS ATTITUDES.*

About two years ago I was discussing Black business ideas with a friend. I blurted out a statement that surprised me with its accuracy. I said to my friend, "You know, White folks go into business to make money whereas Black folks go into business to be the boss." He hesitated a second and then asked me to explain myself. I will try to do the same here.

White folks go into business with the idea that the customer is always right. A customer can complain about price, service, quality or any number of variables and the business owner will simply take it all in, smile and double his or her efforts to improve their service and image. White folks understand that the money is made in having large numbers of customers, and one gets large numbers of customers when he or she is liked. Business people are liked when they break their butts catering to wait on their customers hand and foot. And they must always be ready with a smile, a good greeting and a good "vibe." In a sense, rather than being independent, a businessman is a servant to every customer that comes through the door. In the long process of building his enterprise, he or she kisses a lot of butt. Evenutally they develop the stability, the wealth and the luxury of having workers to take over the operation. The owners require the workers to continue the same service policies. The White businessperson has made his or her money and achieved *real* freedom.

The Black businessperson on the other hand often has gone into business to get away from the kissing butt bit. That is exactly what he or she had to do on his or her old job and even more so because he or she was Black. After they've scrimped and saved and sacrificed enough to open their business, the last thing they are inclined to do is to quietly smile and accept every Tom, Dick and Harry's criticism of their business. The Black man is desperately trying to find some damn place on the planet Earth where *his* or *her* word is law. Most of the time it is at *their* place of business. Thus, when you walk into a Black business you get a greeting if the owner is in a mood to greet. You get a good "vibe" only if the owner isn't pissed-off by something or other. Because the owner is the boss; everything is determined from the vantage point of what serves his personal interests. If he opens and closes at irregular hours (C.P. time), its because he doesn't feel the public should dictate when *he* should open *his* store. His place of business reflects his personal standards in looks, cleanliness, etc., and not necessarily the standards of a man who cares about "what the public will think." Finally, many Black businesspersons are not interested in growing past a certain point, their personal "get by" point. As long as they see themselves reaching their "get by" point every year, then *they* are satisfied. Everything will be judged not on the basis of "will this lead the company to fast growth" but rather "will this get by?" He's not asking his customers "will this get by?"; he's asking himself. Damn the customers. If they don't like it, they can go someplace else. Have you ever heard this in your neighborhood stores? Many of these same persons will complain later down the line about the lack of support they receive from the Black community.

In reality things are not this black and white. The real tragedy is when the number of businesses within easy access to the Black community are owned by crude cold Whites who talk at and treat their Black customers like dirt. They know they can get away with it because Black folks have put up with it for years and still don't have anyplace else to shop. Meanwhile, the crude, rude White owner is taking our money and his vandalism problems lead him to treat all his Black customers as potential thieves.

12. *NON-ACCEPTANCE OF THE DELAYED REWARD PHILOSOPHY.*

The basic reason why people are willing to go through any type of sacrifice is because they believe that the rewards of such sacrifice will be great and will be worth the effort. This kind of person is full of faith in the future. It should not be surprising that Black folks generally have no reason to have this kind of confidence in the future or themselves. We can depend on virtually nothing because we don't control the rules of the society. In many cases after we *have* sacrificed to reach a certain position, White folks change the rules on us and our dreams and faith become a myth or a joke. Many folks of incredible talent and potential say what the hell; live life for today and let tomorrow take care of itself. Black folks have seen how the young and the unsuspecting are knocked down by problems and circumstances that would never have occurred had the person been White. Sacrifice? For what? Delayed gratification? The only thing that has been certain for Black folks is delayed gratification.

I understand and appreciate both the attitudes and the conditions which cause such attitudes. The problem, however, is that no-one else can eliminate risk as a factor of striking it rich in this country. The serious Fortune Builder must sacrifice, must plan for the future and must understand that the real value of their work will only really be obvious at a later time and place. In other words, there *must be* delayed gratification.

SUMMARY

The factors holding Black folks from wealth are much too numerous to be totally listed here. This section is designed to merely give the reader a general feel for the kinds of factors working internally within the people and the community which are keeping many of us from developing to our potential. Most of these internal problems relate to a poor use of time, money, energy and mental concentration. These things we can control ourselves and must learn to control if we are to beat poverty and powerlessness.

I wish to make clear that it was not my intention to draw a stereotype picture of Black failures or shortcomings. I am well aware that White folks *have* every bit and *do* every bit of the self-defeating actions discussed above, so racial characteristics are not the major point at all. The point is that we cannot afford the wasteful activities which we participate in because we are poor and out of power. We are unable to control the major economic factors which control our lives. That is the point. People in power and in the money can and will always be able to tolerate more waste in their lives than the rest of us. We need to be extra critical of ourselves because we should know that the struggle for wealth is not going to necessarily be easy. Therefore, we must examine everything, eliminate all signs of waste and direct our energies to the major task at hand, making money—*period.*

Taking Care of Serious Business

The first three chapters of this volume has hopefully given you a lot to think about in terms of understanding your relationship to wealth. I have tried to answer three fundamental questions:

1. What is wealth and how is it defined?
2. What did the people, who have the money, do to get it? and
3. What's holding us Black folks from getting our share of the wealth?

In answering these basic questions, a lot of principles and philosophical points of view were touched upon. To quickly review my points of view regarding fortune building, it is as follows:

a) I believe that racism is one hell of a consideration and handicap for Black folks in making money in America. But, I do not believe it can stop the majority of Black folks who are determined to make their fortunes.

b) I believe that everyone, Black and White, has to operate in an incredibly complex system of internal and external forces which influence our capacity to make money. Since no one can control the external forces, a person should concentrate on controlling the internal forces relating to oneself. The greater you can control the internal factors, the more effect you can have on the outside world.

c) That attitude is the single most important element in assisting or restraining a person from making his or her fortune. Negative attitudes are rather natural in the Black community for obvious reasons, but there are means for Black Fortune Builders to overcome these attitudes.

d) There are definite methods to building fortunes as there are methods of staying in poverty. I believe that once a person understands these two sets of principles they can unravel the mystery of money and understand that there is no mystique or magic to making money.

e) The final point that has been hit upon, in several different ways, is the extreme importance of the use of time. Time is the most limited asset. Once you waste away big chunks of time, it is lost

72

forever. In this life, you most likely will run out of time before you run out of money.

If you have a general agreement with these principles, then you may be on your way to learning what's necessary to build a fortune. As you may have suspected, however, it is a lot easier to agree on principles than to follow through with plans based on principles.

The chapters which now follow are a little less philosophical and are more closely aimed at outlining a series of plans and procedures to take you from poverty to wealth. I have attempted to explain not only what to do, but I've also tried to deal with perhaps the even more important questions of why. Some of the things I will recommend may sound unreasonable to many of you. It is for that reason that I have taken extra pains to explain why and then leave it up to the reader to make his or her own choices.

UNDERSTANDING THE BASICS

Listed below are several recommendations and explanations which when understood will prepare you to set up an Action Plan. (The Action Plan is the actual step-by-step process which allows one to develop a foundation for serious fortune building projects). Obviously, the information which immediately follows is just a series of brief statements on the topics as each topic could easily become a book in itself. If, however, you leave with a better perspective of the topic and the desire to learn more on each topic, then the intended ends here would have been met.

THE BASICS OF ATTITUDE

Attitude, as I have said before, will probably be the single most important factor of your fortune building plans. What is the proper attitude that one needs to make it through all the changes one has to go through to achieve success? My answer is that there is no one attitude but a whole set of interrelated attitudes. Some (but not all) of the right attitudes are the following:

1. *Make up your mind that you are going to find out pretty quick what you want out of life.* Most of us don't know what we want out of life so it makes it a lot easier for us to accept all the BS that people throw our way. This must be changed. You have

got to determine what you want to accomplish, what it is going to cost and is it worth it. Once you match a goal with a cost and it seems to be worth it, then go for it.

2. *Adopt the attitude that you are building something that will last 'til after you are gone.* In your quest for fortune and whatever else you want out of this life, you will hit an occasional stone wall and it will seem like an impossible barrier to your success. This will be a test of your faith, drive, endurance, guts or whatever. You will ask yourself often, "Is it all worth it?" If what you are trying to do will die when you die, then you may have serious doubts if "it" is worth all the effort, pain and sacrifice. But if what you are seeking to do, to build, will last and benefit others, such as your children, church or community, after you are gone, you will find a way to get around that stone wall. To leave a piece of land, a secure home, a life-supporting business as well as a reputation and an example of strength and independence for others, that, my friend, is something. The attitude is not "getting over" or "getting by" but "building," "building and leaving behind."

3. *Adopt the attitude that life is a numbers game.* I can think of no human enterprise, especially the kinds that are competitive, where numbers are not what really separates the men from the boys. All our lives we play numbers games. We apply for ten jobs so that we might get one. We apply to ten colleges so that we can get accepted by two or three. We shop at several stores but we will buy *one* product in *one* store. Why is it important to adopt the attitude that life is a game of numbers? Because that is what will make us persevere and continue onward after early failures. We reach quality through the examination of quantity. We achieve confidence after we have survived and withstood failures and the test of time. Many success stories will tell you "never give up," "persevere," "don't give up." I think it makes more sense to simply say that you have to adopt the attitude that everything is tied to the numbers game.

4. *Adopt the attitude of persuasive discussion.* There is an old saying that "nothing happens until there is a sale." You may or may not believe that business and the dollar bill is tied to everything, I don't know. But you will have to admit that all of us from time to time engage in the art of persuasive discussion. Persuasive discussion is conversation where one party is trying to convince another party of a fact, idea or product which the listening party is slow, hesitant or resistant in accepting. It could be children being persuaded to eat their food or a woman being asked to bed or a politician being encouraged to sign a bill. Everybody at one time or another is sell-

ing, pushing, advocating, stressing, persuading an idea or product to be appreciated or understood one way rather than another. In that sense, we are all salesmen.

Why is the adoption of this attitude important? Because the difference between successful people and unsuccessful ones, oftentimes, is that successful people take it upon themselves to persuade people through discussion. Successful people try it more often and do it more successfully. If you as a Fortune Builder could just accept the fact that you must learn to improve your powers of persuading persons through discussion, you will find that the whole fortune building process will be easier, and you will be more prone to success than failure. As a Black person you may initially need to practice more persuasive discussion on yourself than anybody else. Why? Because there are incredible negative forces lurking about the ambitious Black man or woman who wants to leave poverty behind and control their life. Friends, family, teachers, White folks, jealous Black women, ego-tripping Black men, etc., all have a laundry list of reasons to explain why you can't do what you're trying to do and why you are crazy. At that point in time, my friend, your attitude, faith and confidence is the only thing on earth that stands between your goals and falling back down in the crab basket with the rest of the crabs. You will need to sit down and do some serious persuasive discussion with yourself to convince yourself that you are right and everyone else, no matter how well meaning, is wrong. You have to sell yourself to yourself and *like* what you're getting.

THE BASICS OF EDUCATION AND RESEARCH

I had a "problem" in elementary school which followed me through high school, college, grad school and law school. The problem never changed much no matter what kinds of students were in my class. Black, White, bright or slow, it was basically the same thing. The "problem" would always involve a "heavy" teacher who would talk non-stop using words, ideas and concepts that you were pretty sure most of the class knew very little about. Year after year I waited for someone to raise his or her hand and say something like, "Hey back up, re-explain everything again and use words we can understand." But it never happened. It became my *job* to raise my hand and ask the kind of questions which usually forced the teacher to slow down, break it down and teach rather than simply run off at the mouth. Many times other students would come up to me after class and say, "That was a real good question you asked; I was wondering the same thing, thanks a lot." At first I was flattered by all these "thank-yous" but by college it was a real pain. I kept asking myself what in the hell is wrong with these other students? If they don't understand the same stuff I don't, why don't *they* ask the damn questions? I get tired of taking the weight for the class to make the teacher teach. So "my problem" was the constant strain of knowing that if I didn't ask the question nobody else would either and I'd never know what was going on. It had very little to do with the other students' intelligence. People just lacked the guts to say, "Hey I don't understand; explain it to me again. It's your (the teacher's) *job* to make sure I know this stuff." I *made* teachers teach me and they usually liked me better for it.

If you have had a "problem" like the one above, consider yourself lucky. You are already in the habit of asking questions and *making* people educate you in what you've decided you need to learn. Making money is not some secret scientific formula, but obviously the information is not widely shared (at least among Black folks) either. The information is simply available. Available to whom, you might ask? Available to those persons, Black or White, who actually chase after the information by running down the right people, asking tons of questions and by simply *making* people teach you what you need to know to make you a fortune. This might sound a little weird, but you just about have to be a pest, a real pain in the ass, who just won't go away until you get what you need.

A lot of people feel they can't or wouldn't do this kind of thing. This is their personal preference. I don't know how they are going to educate themselves, however, because in the real world there are few courses, teachers or text books on the topic of making money. Only you know the questions you have in your head. The most basic idea on education that you could ever learn is simply learning how to open your mouth and ask questions—*your* questions—*period.*

If there are no teachers and if the Black community is full of misinformation, secrecy, envy and other factors negative to clear factual information, who do you ask? Good question. Let us start with the two most basic documents in every city in America: the newspaper and the yellow pages.

I am absolutely amazed sometime to realize how few Black folks read the newspaper. Those that do read the paper read the sports, the funnies, a horoscope, the crossword puzzle and then throw it away. A few more may check headlines, the ads and clip some food coupons. If you are trying to make a lot of money, you need to use your newspaper and make it work for you. Suggestions:

    1. Familiarize yourself with the Business Opportunities section of the paper. It is in the Sunday section of major papers and it lists businesses for sale. If you wanted to go into the greeting card, butcher, ice cream or most other types of business, there is usually at least one for sale listed in this section of the paper. Call up the

owner and express your interest and ask him or her about 7 or 8 quick questions. In five minutes you can learn some important information about the business which interests you, for free, and without leaving your own home. Say you were really interested in a plant shop, bar, liquor store or laundromat and you talked to say 20 different owners over a period of six months. Don't you think you could get a pretty good education about how to make money in that business? And it's all free and right there in the newspaper.

2. What about partners? Say you have $15,000 in cash and you want to do something, but you don't have a clear idea of what. Check the paper. People advertise often under the "looking for serious investor" kind of ad. You see, White folks can meet on a street corner and hook up a deal and make money. Black folks have been so exploited and misused that they may end up trusting only people they were baptized with. The problem is that the people you were baptized with may have no concept of freedom and independence and they'll never have $15,000 in cash in their whole life. So what are you going to do? You may have to go to the end of your rainbow with a blind date. Blind dates are listed in the newspapers. Can you get swindled? Of course you can, but not if you check it out with your team members first. That's what you have them for.

3. The newspapers can tell you who is lending money and how to contact them. Read the legal notices (that's the real fine print that even the White folks skip most of the time) to see how you can pick up a house cheap at a sheriff's sale.

4. The financial section usually announces the start of new federal and state programs, especially those for minorities. What's the use of Black leaders fighting for special programs or the government adopting the programs if the folks don't read the paper to find out the news? Do you think they're going to come to your door with special invitations? The financial sections also has the best ads on sales. But bargains are much better than the department store sales. They are called *Auction Notices* and you can clean up if you ask enough of the right questions and come with money. Very few poor folks go to auctions; you usually see only the middle class. Is this due to prejudice? No! Both groups get the same newspaper and the same notice. One group just continues to go downtown and pay the 100% markup while the other group pays about 50% of true value (or less). Read your paper.

5. The newspaper identifies the experts, the people who know what's happening. That's why they are in the paper in the first place. If after reading an article you have this tremendous question which would clear up a hell of a lot of confusion for you, you have two

choices to pick from. You can call the person quoted in the paper directly and say, "Hey I read your statement in the paper and it was really fantastic (butter them up). But I just have this one question. How do you . . . ?" This person will be so tickled by their moment in the spotlight that they may not shut up. Again you would be getting free consultant service from an expert.

On the other hand, if the person is a real "heavy" and you have to go through three operators to reach their secretary, then use choice number two. Call up the newspaper and ask the guy who wrote the article your question. He may not know the answer, but he may tell you what the expert told him that didn't get into the actual newspaper article.

Do "normal" people do these crazy kinds of things, making all these calls and asking strangers all these questions? Of course not. "Normal" people don't even ask their teacher questions. But then "normal" people have just normal incomes and that is what we are trying to change, right?

6. The Yellow Pages. Basically everything I said about newspapers applies to the yellow pages as well. Everybody in the yellow pages is in the business of making money; that's why they are in the yellow pages in the first place. As experienced businesspersons, they too are experts. All you have to do is pick up the phone, push seven buttons and say, "My name is Joe Blow and I have this problem which you might be able to help me with. I need to know . . ." Every smart businessperson knows that you never really sell products, you sell *the answers to people's problems*. The biggest money to be made is in answering problems.

If you can learn to do the simple procedures above, you can do all the research and get all the education you'll probably ever need in the various stages of your fortune building years. Naturally, boldness is a requirement. Boldness is required to ask the right questions which will get the really meaty answers you are looking for. But look at it this way: If you honestly believe that you should be making 50, 75 or 100 thousand or more dollars a year, and you are Black, you must be a pretty bold person anyway, right? Dig it!

THE BASICS OF A JOB SEARCH

I have not talked very favorably about jobs in this book. This is mainly because I have seen, as you probably have seen, how a job can box people in, cripple their growth and create rather narrow-minded and sometimes paranoid individuals. But almost all of us must start out in some form of a job in our early years. Business and independence takes qualities, assets and circumstances that most of us do not have when we reach maturity and face the working world. Because of these cold hard realities, we must consider the basics of getting a job.

The first thing you as a Black person should understand and be very clear about is this: *There is not and there never will be a job for every American who wants to work.* Understand that. All this bull you have learned from your teachers, local politicians and parents about full employment is a pipe dream. America is a capitalist country where the advantages are on the side of the capitalist, not the worker. Under capitalism it is the desire of the people in power, the bankers, manufacturers, the President and top politicians, etc., to have what is called an "acceptable level of unemployment." They do not want full employment because that would put too much power in the hands of the workers and workers could be in a much better bargaining position for wages. If there were full employment there would be no competition for jobs since everyone would have one. If there were no competition for jobs, the employees could not pretend that workers were a dime a dozen and use the job to control and threaten you like they often do now. If there were full employment or worse, if there were more jobs than people, the employer would need you more than you would need him. How could he grow and develop and beat his competitors if he couldn't hire more workers? How could he hire more workers if everyone was already employed? Even if he could lure workers away from his competitor, wouldn't he or she have to offer more money and benefits and wouldn't that eat into profits? You have to understand that a capitalist looks at workers and money in almost exactly the same light, and why not. Money buys more workers and more workers bring more money. This being so, you have to ask yourself, would a capitalist want to *use up all his capital* so that there would be none left to use when he really needed it for expansion and emergency situations? The answer is an unquestionable No! Now, would the capitalists want to use up all the available workers so that there would be none left for expansion and emergency situations? The answer is another unquestionable No! Just like you want some money in the bank *doing nothing* but laying there in case you need it, the capitalist wants a pool of workers doing nothing but laying there in case they are needed. Besides, suppose there is a war? Who is going to fight the war if everybody's working? If the country is going along at full employment (everybody working) and all of a sudden a million men have to be put into military readiness, don't you think that would put the national economy in a crisis? Does a nation need a national economic crisis precisely at the time it's getting ready for a war? No, my friend, this nation is not, never has been and never will be interested in making sure there is a job for *everybody*.

Right now this desirable or "acceptable level of unemployment" is about 4% of the working population. What does that mean for Black folks? Well, we know that our unemployment rate is always at least twice the figure that it is for White folks. That means at least an 8% unemployment figure for Blacks. We also know that the unemployment statistics only count people *looking for work* as being unemployed. They do not count unemployed people who have stopped looking for work. They do not count prison inmates as being unemployed either. So you add the prisoners to the hopeless and the unemployed and you have a figure that is guaranteed to be at least 10% unemployment for Blacks. This 10% figure is not considered a disaster figure. It corresponds to the 4% (White) acceptable level of unemployment that comes from governmental sources in Washington. What does this all mean? It means, as I said before, that life is a numbers game. There are some people, especially Black folks, who will never have a job just as there are some women (especially Black women) who will never have husbands.

In spite of the gloomy reality of these facts, the other fact is that you have a close to ninety percent chance of getting a job if you practice certain principles. There are countless books on how to get a job; and even though 99% of them were written for White folks, the principles can still be applied to Blacks in most cases. Read at least one of these books if you've had trouble getting a job. Read more than one if you are serious. Every library in America has these books so money should not be a factor.

I will cover here some very basic tips on job hunting.

1. *Know what you're selling before you leave home.* You are a product; you come in a certain size with certain features and you cost so much money. The ultimate question is, "What is the employer buying?" That's correct, buying. The employer is buying your time. What is he going to get for his or her money? The only spokesman for you is you. You have to sell yourself. Every employer needs to see that he's going to get more in return (in work, value, dollars and cents) than he's going to put out. You have to show him how you can make him some money.

2. *Don't ask for charity.* The worse two answers or statements any Black person can give to a potential employer is "I need a job" (so therefore hire me because I need a job) and "I'll do anything." In the first case you're asking for sympathy or charity and employers have little of either. Besides, it's hard to respect a person who asks for charity and I would hope you always want your self-respect. In the second case you must understand that by saying you'll do anything you're suggesting that you *can do* anything. If you could do anything you'd not only already have a job, you'd be so rich you wouldn't even need one. Make sure that you can tell your potential employer what you can do.

3. *Understand the numbers game.* Looking for a job is a full time job. If you really accept the fact that life is full of number games, you will understand that your number is bound to come up. But you have to keep playing. It shouldn't shock you to realize that you may have to ask 100, 150 or more people for a job before you get one. The issue is how long a time will it take you to make 150 stops. To some people that means 150 days because they're only going to ask one person a day. To others that might mean three weeks because they've promised themselves to make 10 inquiries each working day. Getting a job is in the numbers, not in the time.

4. *Try the sex changeover tactic.* There are a lot of small newspaper stories which continue to point out the fact that the line between "mens' jobs" and "ladies' jobs" is quickly disappearing. I doubt if we will ever have female quarterbacks in the NFL or an all-male secretarial staff at a major corporation. But this doesn't mean that over a period of time most of us will find jobs virtually sexless. If you are finding it hard to find the job you really want and in desperate need of something, you might want to apply for a "man's job" if you are a female and vice versa if you are a man. Companies and corporations are very image conscious and they all hate to be sued. Just as they wanted their "token" Negro in the 1960's during the civil rights movement, many want their "token" man or woman in traditional job categories to avoid the label of being sexist. Of course, your own sexuality may be called into question here and the "what will they say" syndrome may be just too heavy to deal with. Obviously if most people are thinking this way, the person who doesn't give a damn what the people say will have little competition and a pretty good chance at getting a job.

5. *Take what you can get and keep searching.* A lot of people will not take a job because they know they wouldn't be happy with it and don't like the idea of changing jobs. To me that's rather dumb. Any job is temporary. Besides, it's easier to demand more money on a job once the employer knows what he's got than to demand decent pay from somebody who sees you as a stranger. Also, the best time to look for a job is when you already have one. People are suspicious of people who are unemployed. They *blame* the unemployed person for being unemployed regardless of how good his excuse for being unemployed. Thus, an unemployed person is looked at as a risk, somebody who might cause problems or leave or steal. But if you already have a job, employers look at you with a little more respect and they have to respect you to hire you. If you are looking to change jobs, then you're viewed as wanting to improve yourself and most people look kindly to that.

Many Black folks have this crazy idea about loyalty to a job.

You want to leave but Mr. Johnson gave you a job when nobody
else would and so therefore, you *owe* him some more time or
whatever. Loyal slaves, that's what I call them. Understand three
things. All employers are getting more out of you than you out of
them so you don't owe them a thing. Secondly, does the loyalty
work both ways? Would he keep you working for him after he
didn't need you anymore because he felt he owed *you* something?
And finally, don't you know that if you died or got sick you could
be replaced in a day or two if the employer wanted to? A lot of
Black folks have a very exaggerated opinion of their value on the
job. It's not that they don't contribute a lot to their work site; it's
just that there are a large number of folks who could do just as well
if given as much time to develop as you have had. It's not worker
replacement that bothers employers; it's the disruption that's the
pain in the butt. Look at it this way. The spare tire in your car
trunk is just as good as any of the other four tires on your car. But
no matter what you're doing, it's always going to be an inconveni-
ence to stop and change your flat tire. Right?

THE BASICS OF BUDGETING YOUR MONEY

Most books teach budgeting by looking forward. I believe in doing it
by looking backward. If you can do it either way, you're on your way.
Let me explain.

Budgeting by looking forward means that a person sits down and
decides what he or she should spend on such items as food, rent, trans-
portation, clothes, etc., and spends just that amount of money and no
more. A regular part of the budget would include a savings payment
which would be that amount of money that a person would deposit in an
account of some kind. Some believe in the "pay yourself first" philosophy.
This idea says that you and your future are more important than any
bill. You deposit your payment (your savings) in the bank *first* and the
expenses comes out of the remainder. Budgeting is influenced by several
factors, such as the level of one's income in relationship to one's responsibilities and dependants and the security of one's employment. More than
anything else, however, it requires personal discipline. It takes a good
deal of discipline to hold tight to the spending limits one sets up because
there always is the temptation to justify to oneself why you are entitled
to go over such limitations. Discipline is something you learn, like anything else, over a period of time and with practice. I believe it's a little
ridiculous to expect a poor person, especially one who has never been
taught budgeting, to all of a sudden muster up all the discipline and

sacrifice necessary to hold the line in obtaining life's necessities. There-fore, I advocate learning to budget by looking backward.

Looking backward means that when you receive your money, you spend it the way that seems to make the best sense to you. After the money is gone you tally up exactly where it all went. You skip virtually nothing. You should be able to see where at least 95% of your dollars have gone. If you must save receipts to remember, then do it. But you must be able to see where the money went. After you have listed where each dollar went, just stop and study it. Look at the list real good and ask yourself the following questions:

1) Where did the money basically go? (Clothes, food, heat, liquor, gasoline)
2) Where is the *waste* in this list? How much was the waste?
3) What things didn't get paid?
4) Is there something which could have been left off and that money better used someplace else?
5) What did I spend on other people?
6) Why did I spend the money I did on the things that I did? Was it just a rare occasion or do I do this all the time?

You can add to this list of questions as much as you wish. By looking backward you are really studying your own spending behavior. You are checking *yourself* out. The whole point of this is for you to be honest with yourself concerning your money. After doing this backward account-ing for a few paychecks you will understand your values and habits a lot clearer because it will be right there in black and white. After you have a real clear understanding of how you *actually* spend money, it will be a whole lot easier to then *plan* how you *want* to spend money. As you make a more determined effort to build a fortune, you will grow in your capacity to discipline yourself and to resist the attempts by others (especially mates and children) to affect how you spend money. My ultimate solution to the budgeting problem will be explained further in the Action Plan.

THE BASICS OF SAVING MONEY

To talk about saving money almost always involves two related, but yet different things. The first idea of saving money means being able to purchase an item for less money than it generally costs to get that same item in most stores most of the time. Most people save money in this way by participating in sales. A store will put an item on sale for many reasons, including fire damage, clearance for new merchandise, change of seasons, holiday, customer competition, etc. The basic purpose of a sale from the store's point of view is to get you in the store, period. The store assumes that once you are inside, you will buy something else other than the sale item, or in addition to the sale item. You could not have possibly bought these other items if they didn't have a way to get you in the store in the first place. This is sometimes called "the lost leader" concept. This means that the store loses money on the sale item but they make it up by the profits on all the other items you buy once in the store.

Sales are a good thing for the sharp buyer who knows a good deal when he sees one (some sale items aren't such a "sale" at all in many cases). But trying to save money strictly through sales means that you are limited to buying at the store's decision and timing rather than your own. Who wants to save money on toys after Christmas? How do you get around the problem of untimely sales? How can you save money most of the time? There are many, many ways to do this. Whole books are available in the library or bookstore on the topic of saving money. If you are seriously interested, go check them out. Here are my ideas on the basics of saving.

1. *KNOW WHAT YOU WANT! (AND IF POSSIBLE, WHY)*

Have you ever noticed that high-powered salesmen never seem to listen to what you say when you're trying to buy something? There is a very good reason for this. You see, many salespersons honestly believe that most people don't ever know what they want, and therefore, you can sell them anything. A large segment of the population often "goes shopping" without the slightest idea of what they need or want. They come home bragging about how they "caught a sale" and pull things out of bags that just kind of blows your mind. If you don't know what you want, go shopping but don't take any money. If it's something that's important or expensive, a day or two of thinking about it will more likely work for you rather than against you. After you've determined what you want, and why you want it, you can then just go pick it up.

2. *AVOID RETAIL PRICES!*

Do you realize that when you pay the retail price on anything, you're paying everybody's salary—the salesman's, the owner's, the wholesaler's, the manufacturer's, the shippers', the insurance man's, the electric company, on and on and on. As mentioned earlier, Black folks need to avoid the local shops, the downtown stores and malls. That eliminates everybody, right? Wrong. There is a wholesaler for almost everything, and many are opening up their own "factory outlet" stores in weird sections of town. The less style, advertising, sales help, and other overhead expenses this person has to pay, the better deal he can give you. It may not be as much fun to shop anymore, but then we are talking about saving money, aren't we?

3. SHOP OUT OF SEASON!

I had stated earlier that nobody wants to buy toys after Christmas. That probably does apply to toys, but not everything else necessarily. It *is* smart to buy at times considered out of season. There are two reasons to buy out of season. First, when the store owner is left with merchandise that is unsold after season, he or she has to make deals to get rid of the leftovers to get what money out of the merchandise that they can get. Out of season is *after* the big clearance sales. Obviously, not everything is sold at the clearance sale; so owners would be even more willing to make deals. In those kinds of situations, many will take what they can get quite often.

The second reason to buy at off season times is that you don't need the items right away. Now this might sound like the opposite of what I said in number one above, but see if you can follow my reasons.

If you live on a very tight budget, needs come first. You buy what you need to get by and only when you really need it. You hope and work for better days. But, if you are doing all right, your needs are being met adequately and you have credit, investments and money in the bank, then a *different set* of rules are used in buying. You buy items in these situations when you are going to need and use the item in the future. Why would you buy something if you didn't need it for six months? Because when you buy something when you need it, you are probably going to pay a lot more for it than at any other time. Why? Because you are *willing* to pay more for it. When you need something right away, you don't stop, compare or hassle over price. You buy it and go on about your business because you're probably pressed for time. But, if you don't need an item right then, you can afford to say, "Hey, I'll give you ten dollars for that thing over there," and see if the owner accepts. He's not going to sell it to anybody else because nobody will be buying those "things" for another six months. He may give you a deal.

4. BUY FROM THE PERSON IN CHARGE!

One of the reasons I don't like to buy things in malls is because there is no room to bargain. You see, there is no one to bargain with. A mall shop hires a high school kid at minimum wage who doesn't know a darn thing about the merchandise. They have no authority to accept any price other than the price as marked. Really, it's only one small step above putting your money in a candy machine. But, when you go to these wholesale type places I was referring to, the owner is right there and you can talk business. "Hi, my name is Sam and this is a real nice place you have here. Look, I need the jacket that goes with these pants, but I'm 15 dollars short according to these price tags. Can we work something out?"

5. *EVERYTHING DOESN'T HAVE TO BE BRAND NEW!*

Does a new hammer hit a nail better than an old hammer? Does a new lamp make a 100 watt bulb give off more light than an old lamp? If your answer to either of the above is yes, we have a real difference of opinion. Most of us are convinced that we need hundreds, maybe thousands of things to live comfortably in this life. The question is does everyone of these things have to come to us in a factory packed cellophane wrapper. Black folks and poor folks in general have a "hand-me-down complex" which started with their parents shopping in thrift shops and the Salvation Army. Others wore clothes that two or more brothers or sisters wore before it got to them. It's understandable why many folks would have a fit at buying anything that was used or secondhand. But, this book is about fortune building and this section is about saving money. You should ask yourself if, in fact, everything you buy *has to be* brand new. If it does, then you may have a head problem deeper than your money problem. The latter may not get straight until the former is seriously dealt with.

6. *LEARN TO USE AUCTIONS!*

You can buy anything, and I mean just about anything, at the right kind of auction. An auction is a signal that somebody's luck has fallen as far as it can go. Somebody has either died, divorced, went bankrupt, or been indicted for a criminal offense. Auctions take place when your situation and your assets are such that you are not to negotiate a normal sale and receive a normal price. Auctions take place when items are of interest to a limited number of people and the only way to bring them all to your doorstep is to have the auction.

In all probability, the absolute best buys are probably to be found at auctions. Why? Because the people determine the price, and it is a complete reversal of roles for customers to tell owners (or their representatives) what they are willing to pay for an important or valuable object. In most instances, owners are forced to accept the best bid and at sophisticated auctions; the very best bid may be only a third of what an object is "truly worth." People at auctions do not buy out of need, so there is rarely *pressure* to have to pay anything higher than a real bargain price. Auctions are listed in the Sunday editions of most major newspapers and can include certain establishments, factories, city-owned equipment, state-owned equipment, vehicles, land, homes and individual or personal property. The worse the weather, the better the auction. Why? because less people show up and the less bidders, the better deal you're likely to get.

7. PAY WITH CASH—BUY IN BULK—CREATE COMPETITION!

There are some salesmen who make their week's pay or their month's pay from one sale. Usually the thing they are selling is either expensive or of interest to only a small number of people, or both. Take cars, for instance. Sometimes a whole week will go by and a new car salesman will have no sale, one sale, or some very low sale figure. This person is very easy to strike a deal with because you might be their only sale that week. Furniture salespersons have a similar situation as do real estate salesmen, computer sales, etc. When you buy a big item, you should be ready with cash and create your own competition. Let me tell you what I did one day.

I got a fat check from a real estate deal and I decided I was going to buy a new Volkswagon Beetle (when they were still considered cheap cars). I went to the yellow pages and listed all the Volkswagon dealers within a fifteen mile radius of where I lived. The next day, I walked into the first car dealer and said,

> "Sir, by five o'clock today, I will buy a brand new WW Beetle with cash money. I know all about the Beetle so all you have to tell me is what is the best price you can give me for today, March 15, 1974."

Most of the salesmen got anxious and didn't know what to say. Others ignored everything this little "colored guy" said and went into their regular spiel. To those, I got up, half smiled, and said, "Good day." To make a long story short, I called one salesman about 4:15 by phone from another dealer and said, "Guess what? You won. I'll be up to see you in a half hour."

I know for a fact that I saved over $500 that day. All because I put the game back on the man. There are plenty of people who pay cash for cars. But, they flash the cash rather than use it to get them folks jumping and falling over each other like they've had Black folks doing all these years.

The same idea can be used in any large purchase. Why pay a higher price and a higher finance charge from the store when you can borrow the money from a bank and pay a lower finance charge and then use the cash to make a better deal. Then you can walk into a store and say,

"Sir, by 5 o'clock today I will have purchased a beautiful new living room, dining room and bedroom set for cash money. I have several places to go before five, and I was wondering what is the best possible deal that you could give me *for today*."

Shopping will never be more fun.

I hope you can understand and appreciate these valuable tips on how to save money on your personal possessions. A second meaning to the idea of saving money is the storing of money. How does one store away dollars in a place like a bank so that it is available for use when needed? It is this form of "saving money" that is the biggest problem for most folks. Let's look at some ways to get around this problem.

SAVING AND STORING DOLLARS

1. *Budget savings.* As mentioned earlier, the most basic idea on saving and storing dollars is to simply "pay yourself first." This is a sound idea for persons who have an adequate income to begin with and who have never had to participate in a struggle for existence during their lives. This, however, would exclude many Black folks because their income, in proportion to their expenses and dependents, is so meager that savings is a real luxury that cannot be afforded.

2. *Added income savings.* Whereas a person may need all of his or her money to survive from one job, a second job should make it possible for at least some money to be put aside regularly as savings. To be unable to do so would suggest a lack of discipline and/or seriousness. More about this in the Action Plan.

3. *The borrowed savings.* Some people are just plain bill conscious. They pay their bills and what's leftover is to be spent enjoying life, period. Sometimes these persons make attempts at saving money and all goes well for a few weeks. Then the pressure of the discipline becomes too great and the money gets spent again. What these folks should consider is a loan-savings account. One simply goes to a bank loan officer and says,

"Look, I've got a decent job, but I have trouble saving money. I'd like to borrow $500 which will be directly deposited in my savings account, and then I'll pay you a monthly payment while my savings earns interest. After a year of paying a certain sum, I'll be so use to paying it, that I'll just put it directly into my account after I pay the bill off."

Most bankers will go along with this idea provided you have decent credit and a reasonably stable job. Banks recognize how hard it is to save in America with thousands of invitations to buy being beamed at you everyday. At the end of a year, you will have $500 plus interest in the bank. But, more importantly, you will have a stronger credit rating and *the savings habit*.

4. *The deducted savings*. There are some people who have such little control over themselves that they feel the only way that they will ever save is to have the money come out of their check before they even see it. There are several ways that this can happen. The first way is to join the company credit union, if one is available, and arrange for a "payroll deduction." When you get your check you will see written in one of those square boxes where certain dollars were deducted and placed in your account in an interest-bearing savings plan with the credit union. This is very simple to do.

A second way may be to join a company pension plan where you can borrow some of the funds during your work years if you desire, or you can let it sit until you change jobs or retire. The problem here is that the pension fund is gaining the additional power from the investment of that money that you could be getting if you had the knowledge and the discipline. But it certainly beats doing nothing.

The third way to have a form of deducted savings is to ask for extra tax money to be deducted from your check every week. At the end of the tax year, when you file your income tax statements, you should be receiving a nice sized lump sum check representing your true tax refund plus your "savings." The government will owe you no interest on this "savings," and they, too, have had the free use of money that you could have been using to build something for yourself. But, this idea at least represents an attempt to budget a savings plan into your life and therefore should be considered.

5. *Company investment savings*. Some private corporations have plans where an employee can invest in the stock of the company. This stock is supposed to be gaining in value as time passes. The money to pay for this stock is deducted from your pay. But, unlike the deductions described immediately above, your money in these circumstances is working for you (and the company). When you leave the company after a certain number of years, you should take away a check (from the sale of the stock) which is a good deal larger than if that money was simply sitting in a bank or credit union. The drawback of saving this way is that often you cannot get at your money too quickly if ever you really needed it. Before you decide on this saving concept, you will definitely want to check with your company to see how long and by what procedure you would liquidate (cash in for dollars) your stock. Another potential danger of this type of plan is that the company's stock may fluctuate (go up and down in value on a weekly, monthly or yearly basis) in value and could be on the weak or down side when you need to cash it in or quit the company. Of course it could go up very high also, and you may have found that your money has doubled or even better. Finally, your com-

pany could go out of business, go bankrupt. In this case you may lose all that you put in. On the other hand, if your company is bought by a larger, stronger company (a book publishing company just bought the New York Mets baseball team last week), the value of your stock is likely to shoot up.

What I have just described in this short explanation here is the basics of what is known in the investment world as the "Risk-Reward Ratio." The risk-reward ratio is very simple: the greater risk of losing one's investment (the greater the gamble, in other words), the higher the ratio of earnings should be if you win. It's like hitting the number or shooting craps.

6. *Personal investment saving.* The purpose of all stored money is to work for you, to earn you more money or value. I have thus far mentioned several savings plans which basically *store* your money. With the exception of the stock plan stated above, these plans involve giving your money to someone else to hold and they invest the money and earn income for themselves giving you a low interest rate in return.

Example: A bank takes $1,000 of your money and pays you 5% interest. The bank then takes that money and gives someone else a car loan or a house mortgage and collects 13% to 17% interest. At the end of the year, they've collected $130-$170 off *your* money and they give you $50 in interest while they walk away with $80-$120. Did you really make $50. No, because Uncle Sam says you owe him tax on that "earning." If you make about 15K per year and pay 25% in income taxes (after deductions), you end up paying the government $12.50 of your $50. If you have to pay state income tax in your state, you will end up receiving less than $35 of your $50. Thirty-five dollars represents a net of 3.5% return on your money. Now, if inflation is 12% (higher in the Black community because we catch everybody else's inflation charges), in terms of the increased cost of living in America, that means that your $1,000 is now worth only $915 in buying power. Check the numbers brother.

$1,000 cash + $35 " real interest = $1,035. Inflation at 12% means you need 12% more ($120) to buy the same goods that cost a grand the year bfeore. With $1,035, you are $85 short of the $1,120 you need to buy $1,000 worth of stuff. Being $85 short is just like having $915 ($85 short) the first year. Dig it?

Now you see why rich folks—smart rich folks—do not keep their money in the bank. When was the last time you were standing in line at the bank and you saw somebody in a Rolls drive up and stand behind you to put his mailbag full of money in the bank? Huh?

You might think that banks are ripping you off; but before you cop an attitude against them, consider the pension fund bosses and *their* situation. In order to really appreciate their situation, you have to understand a couple more facts about savings. America is among the lowest ranking White countries in the world in terms of worker savings. A worker in the U.S. who makes say 10K a year will save 5.6% of that or $560 (about $11 a week) a year. Most of the time, this saving is *voluntary* and the money is deposited in a bank where you have *free access* to the money by way of checks, withdrawals, etc.

But, in many, many jobs you are "forced" to contribute to the pension fund as long as you are on that job and the amount of money they *take out* is often more than 5.6%. They then take this money and often make more money than the banks. How? Check this.

When a business needs to expand or otherwise is in need of cash, they go to a bank and apply for a loan. Because the banks have such strict guidelines, businesses often get turned down. Where else can they go to borrow money? They can go to the public (sale of stock), insurance companies (they are a whole different story), or to pension funds. Now, if a bank turned a business down for a loan, there must be a high risk associated with the project, right? And if there is high risk, then there must be a high reward (because that's the risk-ratio rule) in return. Therefore, the pension fund charges a higher interest rate to the business borrower than what the bank would charge. Let's say they charge 18%. At the end of the year, the pension fund has $180 profit for every $1,000 which they "forced" you to put in. When you finally leave the company in five or ten years, they give you your money back but something will be missing. The thing you would be missing is purchasing power. You may have put in $5,000 and gotten back say $6,000, but that $6,000 will buy less when you get the check than at any other time in all the years that you've been working at the company. Fortunately for the pension fund bosses (but bad for you), you are so excited and thrilled about having $6,000 in one lump sum that you don't know and don't care how you've been ripped off. If you're a fool, you take the money and blow it all on foolishness. If you're average, you'll put it in the bank and get ripped off once again.

What's a poor Niggra to do? Get smart and participate in *your own* investment savings. Make your money make more money.

How does one make one's money make more money? Simple. The answer is *not* making the money make more *money* but using the money to obtain assets that grow in value or assets where *you add* the value. Are you confused? Good, that means you will read this next paragraph slowly and carefully.

In the business world (the real world), there is a term, a concept, called "Appreciating Assets." For all practical purposes, *appreciating* means "gaining in value." The way a person makes "money" from his or her invested savings is to not concentrate on always getting the *dollars* in their hand at the end of every year, but to concentrate their attention on the gain in value of the things they own. When do they actually get the dollars in the hand? They get it whenever they decide to sell the thing that has gained in value. This means the savings investment dollar is used to buy something and the money doesn't actually get to you until after the thing is sold.

What types of things are considered appreciating assets? Here are a few examples: 1) land; 2) houses and other types of real estate; 3) gold; 4) silver; 5) diamonds; 6) valuable art; 7) antique furniture and housewares; 8) rare coins; 9) rare stamps; 10) antique cars; 11) other valuable stones and metals.

There is a category of items which could go up in value but could also stay the same or go down, and these include: 1) real estate; 2) stocks; 3) boats; 4) fur coats; 5) cars; 6) businesses; 7) airplanes, etc.

Each one of the things listed above is a whole area of study. Investing can be not only a means of making money but can be quite exciting and fulfilling as an activity or hobby also. You might get excited over a slam dunk or a touchdown; but a stamp, coin or art collector "freaks" when he or she gets wound up in his or her thing. Obviously the knowledge, care and level of investment-saving dollars required to get involved in these things is a great deal of the reason why so few people, even White folks, get involved in this kind of thing. But making money in this country has always taken a specialized degree of knowledge, the ability to weigh risks and the right kind of dollars to invest (save).

It would be especially easy to see why Black folks would not be particularly involved in some of these enterprises because it comes down, in many cases, to a knowledge or *love* of European history, values and culture. Valuable stamps, in many instances, are European stamps; and the same can be said for the coins, art work, furniture and housewares. In the Black community, something is either old fashioned or modern. The fact that something has a Gothic, French Provincial or Victorian style means very, very close to absolutely nothing.

What kind of "return" (gain in value) can be expected from these appreciating assets? The answer to that question is extremely complex. Take gold for instance. They say gold goes up in price when there is uncertainty or danger in the world. How much danger equals how much return? No one knows and no one can predict. These appreciating assets are basically not in your control or power to determine. The term used for this is "speculative." It's anybody's guess. But one thing is usually pretty certain—regardless of how good or bad things can go, one is pretty certain that after his or her sale is made, the return will be better than the bank's or credit union's 5 or 6%. Also, if you have kept the item for over a year, you pay a *capital gains tax* rather than an *income tax*. Let me explain.

Say there were two guys, Phil and Bob, who each paid $2,000 of their $10,000 incomes to taxes every year. Each guy got a $5,000 check that they received in a car accident settlement and they were looking for a way to save-invest it. Phil puts his in the bank and gets 6% interest for one year. His interest is $300 for the year. Since he pays taxes at the rate of 20% (2K is 20% of 10K), he must pay $60 (20% of $300) to taxes. He pays at an *income* tax rate.

Bob puts his $5,000 into one painting. He brings it home and hangs it in his living room. At the end of the year, Bob's painting is now worth $6,500. Bob decides he wants to buy a different painting, so he sells his investment. His profit from the sale is $1,500. Now you would think that Bob would pay $300 (20% of $1,500) in taxes wouldn't you? That is not so, however, because Bob pays capital gains taxes, not income taxes. Technically, the law says that he doesn't earn his living buying and selling paintings. Bob would pay taxes on only 40% of his gain and he would pay only his normal rate of 20% on that. Dig it? $1,500 × 40% = $600. Bob pays taxes on $600. How much tax does Bob pay on $600? Bob pays 20% or $120. How much does Bob make from his painting? He makes $1,500 minus taxes of $120, resulting in a profit of $1,380. Bob would have had to have over $287,000 in the bank at 6% interest to make as much money as he did hanging that picture in his living room for a year. Bob couldn't have put that much money in the bank anyway; not if he had any sense. Why? Because banks will only insure 100K of anybody's money in an account. So, why should you deposit 280K if you could only get 100K back if something happened. You see, not even banks expect (or want) people to put large sums of money in their accounts. Bob would have had to open up accounts in three banks to hold that amount of money.

7.   *Added value savings-investment.*   Most of the investment items mentioned above can lead you to the pot of gold at the end of the rainbow. But as an investor, you have no control over how long it's going to take or how much you are going to make. No one can control the price of gold and other valuables. No one can predict accurately if an up and coming artist's work will double, triple or quadruple in value in two years or ten years. The information and control factors are so complex and specialized that you almost have to dedicate yourself to be an expert to be sure you'll be on the gravy train.

Value added types of savings-investment are slightly different. You have some common knowledge and *control* over what will happen and you can predict how much return you will get back from your efforts. It takes work to *add value* to make a thing appreciate and you know how people feel about work. Let's look at a few examples.

James took mostly auto shop courses in high school and by the time he got out of the Army, he could not only fix most things on most cars, but he could customize cars very creatively. James knows the value of cars. He knows the prices for parts and labor that most repair shops charge, and he can come on as a pretty strong salesman when he wants too, also. When a guy complains about how he's tired of pouring money into his car, James is quick to check the car out and make an offer to purchase the thing. He never buys the car unless he knows several things.

A. That the price he's paying is a real deal regardless of what has to be done to the car.

B. That he can repair whatever is wrong with the car himself.

C. That he knows how he wants to customize the car, how much it will cost and what it will sell for.

D. That it will sell within a certain period of time and he has a pretty good idea who would probably be interested in buying the completed car.

Now in this situation, James has almost total control of everything. He controls the price in a sense because he doesn't have to buy if it's not a good deal. Secondly, he has control over the cost of repair. As an expert, he can do the work himself and most definitely get parts at a cheaper price. He can plan and predict how much the repair job will cost him.

When the car is customized, James is not only adding value based on the improvements being made, but he is adding value with the creativity and the uniqueness of its design. Creativity and uniqueness add big bucks to anything from the ring on your finger to the skyscraper office building downtown.

Finally, James is knowledgeable of the market. He knows the car will not be sitting around gathering dust because people come to him all the time to see what car he's working on.

Let's look at how an added value deal, in this case with cars, might work.

The car is bought for $500. The car costs $71 in repair parts and $350 in customized materials. James uses 27 hours of his time and the car sold for $3,000. Now, you can look at this thing two ways.

#1 Total Cost = $500 + $71 + $350 = $921

$3,000 − $921 = $2,079 ÷ 27 = Jim made $77 per hour for every hour he put into adding value to the car.

Looking at it a different way, you could say this.

#2 Total material cost − $921

Total labor cost − 27 hours × $15 = $405

Total cost = $921 + $405 = $1,326.

James *added value of $1,674 over the cost of time, labor and materials.*

If you can't fix cars, boats or planes, restore furniture or repair old home appliances, you may think you're out of luck. But, could you learn to paint walls? How many walls do you think you could paint? Enough to make up a room or a house? The cost in labor and parts to paint a square foot is about $.08. The added value is about $.25 a square foot. Now, if you could buy about 8,000 square feet of walls that needed painting and then sold 8,000 square feet of newly painted walls, you could clear about $1,360 (8K × 25¢ − 8K × 8¢). The best way to find unpainted walls is to find an old house that needs painting. Buy it and paint it.

Before wrapping up this brief overview of savings, there are several points which I think must be made. First, regardless of what kind of way you choose to save or invest your money, you have got to keep some cash savings where you live. Why? Because the best time to have money is when you need it. And it seems like accidents, sickness, visitors, sales and special events mostly happen on weekends and at night when banks are closed. It will not help you at all to have all your money tied up in banks, stocks, rare coins, or custom cars if the baby is sick and needs three prescriptions costing sixty-one dollars. If the oil or gas furnace breaks down, you can get somebody out to fix it. But they will probably take no checks or credit cards. All the appreciating assets in the world won't get that house warm. Only cold cash will do. If you don't keep some cash around your house, you better have the phone number of a good friend that does.

Secondly, you should see by this point that there is no one answer as to how to store your money. For example, everybody should not only have *some* money in the bank, but they should have some money in several banks. The more banks you deal with, the more bankers you'll know and the better your credit report looks. The more branches you use, the less running across town you have to do to "catch the bank before it closes." Even in terms of writing checks for bills, it's a lot easier if you write from one bankbook a month and another bankbook the next. This gives all your checks time to come back. That way your checkbook won't constantly be saying one thing while your bank statement says something else, and you're pulling your hair out to see what the foulup is.

Finally, there is a question that always seems to come up when people discuss saving, and it is this: Do I start saving before I pay off my bills, or do I pay off my bills first and then save? I believe strongly in consolidating your bills (make many bills into one large bill through a debt consolidation loan) and start saving (or investing) immediately. Why? Because it is important to establish the savings *habit* as soon as possible. If you wait until this mysterious date in the future, when all your bills are paid off, you may find that date never coming. Most of us will always have bills. So, start saving now. Pay yourself first.

THE BASIS OF CREDIT DEVELOPMENT

The idea of credit, people borrowing money or materials from other people or institutions, is a concept that has been around for a long time. Being in debt, however, was looked upon negatively for most of recorded history. People always desired to be debt free. "I don't owe anybody and don't want to owe anybody" was the popular wisdom which most Black folks learned from their parents and grandparents. Southern Blacks especially had been exploited to the most ridiculous degree by White folks who historically kept them in perpetual debt to keep them working the cotton fields in systems known as "share cropping" and "tenant farming." In Northern cities deceitful merchants used all kinds of outlandish credit contracts to make poor folks pay for furniture and household appliances at least twice before they could fully claim ownership. If you combine these bad experiences with all the many reasons, excuses and justifications that banks have given Black folks for not lending them money, you can easily see why Black folks have never had a chance to appreciate the benefits of good credit.

America, however, has evolved into a do-it-now pay-for-it-later type of nation. The captains of industry have always assumed that the average consumer would not spend over their heads. People were expected to gain in job salary and security over a period of time. There was to be little worry about debts being unpaid.

In spite of racism, many Black folks in recent years have had a chance to get involved in the buy-now-pay-later economy. As a consequence of these credit temptations, thousands and thousands of Black and White folks got in debt over their heads and have had all kinds of negative experiences as a consequence of this overspending.

Many Black folks thought they were upwardly mobile and spent their money accordingly. Many found out that the last hired executive is the first fired executive just as it is in the ranks of the workers.

Many Black folks don't want credit cards, overdraft privileges or anything which they interpret as getting them into a financial trap. Most folks, however, who find themselves paying cash for everything did not give up on credit; credit gave up on them. The "pay all cash" consumer who has ruined his credit rating due to unpaid bills does not really understand how they are trapping themselves into a lifetime of virtual poverty and powerlessness.

The truth is that credit is very much like any powerful tool—it can work tremendously for you or against you depending on what care and use *you* give it. The need for credit is almost certain for anyone interested in building a fortune. You know it takes money to make money. What you don't understand, perhaps, is that *first* money is almost always somebody else's and you need good credit to get it. Even if a person were to start a business on their capital, before you could lease a building, apply for bonding, get insurance or purchase needed machinery, your credit would be checked out a half a dozen times or more. If you accept the fact that developing your credit worthiness is a non-negotiable necessity to building a fortune, then you will get further faster. But if you struggle against the tide and fight dealing with this aspect of your personal profile, you will simply prolong the process and waste a lot of time and effort.

Actually, understanding credit is not hard at all so this section might sound like something you have read or heard before. It is the discipline that people find hard to deal with. The information below is divided into three parts. The information from one may be relevant to the other parts also. Part one deals with how one begins a credit history if they do not have one presently. Part two deals with how to straighten out your credit if you have fallen behind or ducked payment of your bills. Part three deals with credit expansions, meaning, how to make the money available to you grow.

DEVELOPING A CREDIT HISTORY

The person who has no credit history at all is usually someone who who has paid cash in the past for all of their major items. Or it could be a person who is just entering the working world. The first thing you must know before establishing credit is to understand what the creditor is looking for when they are reviewing applications and why.

On the credit application, you give the creditor hints as to whether you are a good risk or not. Let's look at what they ask and why.

1. Address and how long at the address. There has been evidence that many stores and other places of business have discriminated against persons who live in a certain zip code because this section of town is known to be poor and historically filled with bad credit risks. This is illegal and if you suspect this may be the case with you, you must report them to the Civil Rights Commission or Better Business Bureau. You can also tell the credit manager directly that you suspect that this is what they are doing and you will report them unless they explain to you why you were turned down for credit.

More important than where you live is how long you have lived there. People who move from place to place often are difficult to collect money from. Many move specifically to get away from bill collectors. Frequent moves are viewed as negative. You will be asked if you own or rent your residence. The reasoning for this question is related to the first; it is a check on your mobility. If you rent it means you are more likely to move than if you owned your own place. Also, if you owned your place you have most likely established some type of credit with someone else since people usually don't pay for their homes in cash.

You will be asked how much rent or mortgage you pay. This will be asked to help determine your *disposable income* which is the income remaining after you have paid your bills. Rent or your mortgage payment is perhaps your biggest expense. A question on utilities may be asked to get a better idea of your living expenses and disposable income.

2.   You will be asked what you do for a living, how long you have been there and what salary you are earning. This is asked for obvious reasons. The creditor wants to know your stability. Some jobs are obviously temporary or seasonal. This is a negative factor when trying to establish credit. Finally, how long you have been working is crucial. Creditors are not going to grant a big loan if the position is not secure or the consumer is still on a probationary period with his employer. Employment for a year is minimal in that it establishes that the job is not seasonal and probably not temporary either.

3.   You will be asked for a bank reference and the account numbers for checking and savings. A person with no bank reference gives the impression that they spend money as fast as they make it. Having no bank reference is usually interpreted as a negative factor. How many other expenses or obligations do you have? This question again gets at the *disposable income* inquiry. Creditors don't want to feel that you have to squeeze all your pennies to make sure everybody gets paid. If they feel you have enough bills already, they will tell you you were denied credit because you were *sufficiently obligated*. If they see you owe no one (you have no other credit established), they will understand that they are the guinea pig and will have to give you your first credit test. This is a negative factor also, believe it or not. Creditors do not like to deal with "virgins" as it cannot be predicted what they will do. Therefore, they constitute the greatest risk. A co-signer may be asked for.

Other questions such as number of dependents, alimony or child support payments to be paid out or received are all addressed to the number one concern of disposable income.

After you fill out the form, you wait for your answer which will either be yes-accepted, no-unacceptable or co-signer needed. The greatest source of information on why there is a rejection is the credit manager. Do not merely accept a *no* answer and let it drop at that. Find out why. Make him or her *explain* the reason to your satisfaction. Listen to the answer. If it sounds on the up and up, they are in fact telling you what you need to do to get your act together. If the answer sounds flaky, then tell him that unless he or she comes up with a better or clearer answer, you will go to his supervisor or the company headquarters to get a better answer. Let it be known that the proper authorities will also hear of your dissatisfaction. This may make a change in the manager's attitude or they may say rather quickly, "bring in a co-signer."

A CO-SIGNER

A co-signer is simply someone who signs all the legal documents that you do and in effect says, "If this person doesn't pay the bill, I will." Many Black folks have trouble getting co-signers, but usually there is a quick solution to that. Buy one. I've been saying all along what kinds of things money can do and one thing it may do is help establish your credit. Offer someone $20-$50 for cosigning your note. Many wishy-washy people will stand at attention and march right down to the store with you if they know you are on the level. You shouldn't have to do this too many times before your name will stand on its own. I've said credit is important. If you accept that, then you should be willing to pay for it by paying someone to help you get yours established.

CENTRAL CREDIT BUREAU

Most sections of the country have a centralized credit bureau. Where I live it's called T.R.W. It is the function of this bureau to keep a record of all the credit transactions of individuals who apply for credit at *member business establishments*. In other words, if Joe's corner grocery store gave you credit, it probably would not show up on the credit sheet from the central bureau. Joe's grocery probably isn't a member who pays a monthly fee to get reports on his customers. A shoe store in the shopping mall probably *would be* a member.

Once you have established credit at a number of major places, this bureau will notify all who inquire about you if given your permission. This allows stores to get a more reliable report on you than what is asked for on the application. As a matter of fact, if what is given by you on the application differs too much from what is on the central credit report, they can deny you credit. In a sense the credit bureau is like a "lie detector test" when compared with your application.

WHERE DO YOU APPLY FOR CREDIT?

When new in the credit game, there are places more likely to extend credit to you than others. Obviously the situations will differ widely depending on local conditions.

1. The place where you work. If you work in a store or other type of place that extends credit, start here; you should get a play. If not, try the credit union for a small loan; they could be very helpful.

2. The place where you bank. Savings is related to credit. If a bank manager can see that you have a small sum of some sort in your savings

account, he or she can feel a lot more confident in granting you checking, overdraft or credit privileges. Remember to use each denial as an opportunity to learn more. Ask the credit manager why you were turned down and, more importantly, what would you need to get approval the next time.

3. Local department stores. Local stores charge a high rate of interest. Part of the reason for this high rate is to cover the losses they encounter on the people who slip out of town. This means that they are prepared to take on risks, especially since the customer covers the costs of the losses. Apply here.

4. Finance companies. Finance companies charge the highest rates of interest. They require some form of security and/or a co-signer. Use these guys only when absolutely necessary. Often the best "line" to give them is your intention to use the money as a debt consolidation loan. This means you are going to pay off your outstanding loans and bills with other places and make one large payment to them. They respond well (in fact everybody responds well) to this type of loan because it means they will be first in line for payment and there will be no other bills competing for the payment money.

STRAIGHTENING OUT "BAD CREDIT"

Let's say that you had more trouble paying creditors than finding them and you find yourself hiding and ducking collection agencies and the like. What do you do? Basically the answer is quite simple. You stop running and make an effort to reach out to the stores, banks and collection agencies to whom you owe money and ask for a truce, a pow wow or conference. You tell the creditors you are ready to pay your bills and that you are interested in cleaning up your credit history. Arrange a payment schedule that is realistic; stress this to the store. Don't promise to pay thirty dollars a month if all you can pay is really fifteen. It is the regularity of payments, not the amounts that are most important. Some people feel that if they pay $100 to a store that "that should keep them quiet" and feel then that they can skip a couple of month's payments. This is not how it works at all. A creditor is interested in regularity, dependability and consistency because that's what his creditors want and he pays them with your money.

How do you know which bills to pay first if you owe a lot of different places money? There is an easy answer to this question and it is this: Apply for credit at a new store. If your credit is bad the store will turn you down. After they turn you down, you are then eligible to apply for a copy of your credit report from the central credit bureau. (Find out their address and send a dollar for a copy of the report.) Once you get the report you will be able to read what the stores have been reading about you. You may find that some bills you owe are not even on the sheet. Other creditors may have made more of the fact that you were repeatedly late than the fact that you were behind in payments. In any event, by looking at this report you can see which places and which statements are causing the most negative response to your application. Obviously these are the bills that you pay back first.

It may be difficult to pay money to a store or establishment if you feel you were cheated on the merchandise or the merchandise was repossessed. Make the best arrangements you can to get a square deal for yourself in terms of the merchandise being paid for. The important thing, however, is not the merchandise itself but your name, your credit record. You will need this to make money in the future. Even if you pay out a few thousand dollars for merchandise that you don't even own anymore it will be well worth it. Why? Because a year or two later you might be able to make all of that money back in a month based on a credit rating that allows you room to wheel and deal. With that bad rating hanging over your head, you won't be able to do too much of anything.

EXPANDING YOUR CREDIT

The kind of credit that we as Fortune Builders are interested in is cash credit. It does us no good to be able to buy a thousand dollars worth of dresses or shoes from a department store if what we really need is a thousand dollars in cash to swing a deal. What this means is that we have to focus our attention on banks since they are the instituitons in existence to lend money. Our concern here is with the two principle means of borrowing money from a bank. The first is the credit card, usually Master Charge or Visa. The second is the checking account overdraft. The overdraft is simply the result of a signed agreement between you and the bank which says that you will be allowed to write checks that are up to $500 (or whatever the amount is) more than the amount you actually have in your checking account. Such an amount will be treated as a loan and you will pay a monthly payment to repay the loan or lose the privilege of the overdraft account. Thus, if you have $500 in your checking account you will be able to write a check up to $1,000 and it will not bounce.

The credit cards are used for the purchase of merchandise or cash advances. Each card has a limit of say $500 for new card holders and up to $2,000 or more for old established (or high salaried) customers. When you need a cash advance you simply walk into *any bank* that honors the credit card and borrow any amount up to your credit card limit.

When most people apply for a credit card or overdraft checking, they simply accept the minimum limit that the bank offers them. A Fortune Builder tries to negotiate through persuasive discussion a higher amount based on need. A person might say any of the following:

1. I'm expecting a baby in May and I'd like to have the assurance and security of knowing that I'll be able to get all the necessities. I was wondering if you might extend my credit card to $1,000.
2. Our family is going to California this summer for our vacation and we need more access to credit. I was wondering . . .
3. The stereo system I want costs more than my credit line here at the bank. The store has offered me the use of the finance company they deal with but I'd rather pay the lower interest rate here. I was wondering . . .

Use your own creativity and personal situation but negotiate the bigger credit line. The secret, of course, is not to wait until you actually need the money.

Sometimes a bank will raise your credit line with a credit card as a result of a good payment record. Five hundred dollar jumps are quite common. Other factors influencing the raise in credit would be the amount owed in other bills, the amount of money you make per year and all the other factors which go into credit analysis.

Ok, say you have found a bank which has given you $500 in checking overdraft, $500 in Visa and $500 in Master Charge for a total of $1,500 in cash credit. You are seeking more. What do you do? Simple. Go to another bank and start all over again. How long can you do this? Well, that varies tremendously and it doesn't serve any purpose to try to put a limitation on what's possible. I can tell you this, many people have four or five Visa cards and Master Charge cards. That's not that unusual. The real question is how much credit does one have in proportion to their salary. Most personal finance books suggest that 30% of one's salary is a good credit resource. That means if a person earns 10K per year, he can get $3,000 in cash in a day's time. I personally think people should push to get access to 50% of their salary while the ambitious should strive to do better.

I personally have obtained credit lines of over 100% of my former salary in cash credit.

Everytime you get a raise or a major event like buying a home occurs, go back to all your credit sources and ask for more money. It should be backed up by a good reasoning, a good payment record and a relationship of some kind with the credit manager. Then go into your "persuasive discussion."

I've recently bought a house and with the price of fuel going up so often it's really hard to budget for home heating oil. I was wondering if you could extend my line of credit?

THE BASICS OF TAXES

The tax field is a truly involved one and is one of the areas that should truly be left to the specialists at a certain point in time. Until that time (which it will after you go into business or own extensive real estate), however, the basic principles are pretty simple.

1. A person does not want to duck paying taxes because that is illegal. One wants to reduce the tax money that one has to pay the government out of one's *own pocket*. The principal method of doing this is through real estate and business deductions. I will not go into business deductions in this volume because they could be quite confusing and contradictory.

2. The real estate means of paying lower taxes operates basically this way:

A person has an income of 24K per year and pays taxes of say $6,000 per year. He or she wishes to pay less tax but does not wish to change any part of their life-style or apartment living. What do they do?

a) They buy a four family house at 50K with a downpayment of 5K and a remaining balance of 45K to be paid off over 30 years at a 13% interest rate. The interest rate is the charge that a lender will charge you for lending you the money. (Although the interest rate is shown as a percentage, most people want to know in dollars and cents what the loan will cost them. This is easy to get, just add up all the monthly payments and get a total. Subtract the original amount borrowed from your total payments and the remainder is how much the loan will cost you in dollar and cents. It is not at all unusual for a 30K house to cost the homeowner 100K after all the payments are added up over 25-30 years.)

b) A landlord is allowed to deduct the expenses of owning and maintaining a building from his profits. Whatever profit is left is what he or she is to pay taxes on. The kinds of things our investor can deduct are:

    Interest paid on mortgage loan

    Taxes paid to the city

    Utility and heating costs

    Management cost

    Repair cost

    Depreciation costs (explained later)

c) Suppose our investor collects $250 a month in rent from each apartment or $1,000 a month, or $12,000 a year. It is reasonable that at the end of one year that person may have a:

$ 5,000	Interest payment deduction
2,500	Tax deduction
2,500	Heating costs deduction
500	Repair costs deduction
700	Management costs deduction
800	Gas & electric utility cost deduction

$12,000	In costs
2,000	In depreciation (explained later)

$14,000 In total deductions.

d) Our investor's income picture looks like this:

$24,000	Job income
12,000	Rental income
$36,000	Total income

—14,000 Deductions

$22,000 Taxable income

Because our investor dropped $2,000 in income "on paper" due to his deductions, his income tax *rate* dropped also. Instead of paying 25% of income to federal taxes, they may now only pay 20% of the income to taxes. Twenty percent of $22,000 equals $4,400. Our investor here has saved $1,600 in taxes and it did not cost him or her a penny because all the expenses were paid by the tenants rent money and all work was done by the management company whose fee was tax deductible also. Depreciation will be explained later.

If our apartment dweller owned another property like this one, his or her taxes would be reduced even more.

One way a person knows if he or she has invested in enough real estate is to see if they have enough deductions to bring their taxable income figure down to the poverty level of 5-7,000 dollars. If they do that, they will owe hardly any taxes at all. If they owe hardly any at all, then all the tax money they have paid in from their salaried jobs will come back to them in *one big check*. Check it out.

THE BASICS OF RECORD KEEPING

The thing which is being pursued by the Fortune Builder is wealth, i.e. money. In order to get it we have to follow its path, track it and record it. We follow the flow of money to see *how* it flows. The more we know about how it flows, the more we can control its flow and the more we can use it to do what we want it to do. We do this by keeping good records. What kinds of records? Let's see.

1. We would want to record our bills to see which ones are rising and which ones are falling and how much we owe out to other people and institutions. In looking at the records of our bills we may see a way to consolidate some of them and pay out less in bill payments every month. Budgets are based on the records of our bills.

2. We would want to record our access to cash credit. Why? Well, why should be negotiate so hard to get access to money for those special occasions and not even know how much you have access to when those occasions actually arise? In any particular week you ought to be able to say to yourself, "If I lost my job tomorrow I know I could get my hands on $4,000 (or whatever the figure) to tide me and the family over until I was able to get another job.

3. We would want to record our income tax deductions. Trying to gather the records to figure income tax deductions just before April 15 can be a maddening experience if you have not been keeping them all along. If the I.R.S. ever calls you down to question a tax return form, they will want to see records in black and white—period. The inability to produce them will probably mean you will have to dig down deep into your pockets and hand over some cash. You don't want to do that, do you?

4. We would want to keep records of the value of our assets. If wealth is more related to the value of our assets than how much we made per week, then we would have to know the value of our assets to know how wealthy we were. Knowing the value of your assets also lets you know how much money you could possibly get if you had to in an emergency situation.

5. We will want to keep a record of our resources. Each Fortune Builder has the responsibility to record his or her own list of important people, agencies, services, discount houses, etc. When the need arises you should be able to reach who or what you want at a moment's notice. As you move through life you will undoubtedly meet some amazing people who may be quite open to working with you. You must record their name and a way to get in touch with them. Some people keep a pile of business cards, others use an address book. I personally keep a notebook. Whatever way you do it just make sure you can get to what you need when you need it.

6. We will want to keep a record of our plans. Many of us have plans to do a multitude of things in this life but most of us never write our plans down. There is something very serious going on when a person actually sits down and records what they intend to do. The very act of writing plans out forces you to come to grips with reality. You ask yourself, "Now is this really possible or am I just kidding myself?" Most

people who take their thing seriously, architects, scientists, football coaches, military generals, teachers and anybody else we can think of, use written plans. These plans tell the actor not only what he or she must do but in many cases how or what it takes to get it done.

If you take your life and your Fortune Building ideas seriously, you must write it down and look at it. Look at it every week or month. Add or subtract from your ideas but keep the written record in front of you. By repeatedly reviewing the written record of your plans, you work on your motivation, your creativity, your mental vision (which helps you to write out even better plans) and a whole list of other things necessary to achieve your goals. Most of this activity could not happen if your goals and plans always remained as a vague set of ideas roaming around in your head.

THE BASICS OF TIME CONTROL

To be time conscious is to be *deadline* conscious. When most of us were young we had deadlines imposed on us by authority figures such as parents, teachers and the like. Homework was due by a certain time, and term projects were due at another. We were told when to be home and by what time the dishes must be washed, our room cleaned or the lawn mowed. Deadlines created pressure, and pressure is something most of us would rather live without. It should be of no surprise then that most of us consider one of the big payoffs of being an adult is the fact that except for our employers, very few people are in a position to impose deadlines and the resultant pressure on us as was done when we were kids. We feel much freer when we can tell everybody that we will do favors or tasks *when we feel like it*. The problem with many folks is that they overreact to childhood problems. In so doing, they develop attitudes which are negative to their development as adults. Attitudes about deadlines and pressure is one such instance of negative attitude development. I think most of us forget that we accomplished tremendous things under pressure. We also forget that some of our greatest feelings of personal pride were the result of having performed well under pressure. But somehow as adults we adopt the attitude of, "I don't want to be pressured into anything."

When we were in school and we *had* to learn the Gettysburg Address by memory or suffer the consequences (a bad grade, a kicked butt, etc.), what happened was that we learned the Gettysburg Address—period. As adults you may now look back at that and ask yourself, "How in the world did I do that?" You did it because you were pressured into it. Someone told you that you *had* to do a thing *by a certain time* or it would be too bad for you.

As a person dedicated to making money, you have to ask your mind and your body to reach their peaks to serve *your* ends. You have to set goals and set a *time limit* within which that goal is to be accomplished. You must put pressure, time pressure, on yourself. Most successful people are successful not because they really care about what other folks think but because it is critically important to them to achieve their own goals within the time frame they have laid out. Hell, anybody can make a hundred thousand dollars; just work 15-20 years at the minimum wage. But to make a hundred thousand dollars within *one year* is significantly more difficult. A Fortune Builder needs to be conscious of various periods of time. While it is true that it takes time to achieve great things, great things do not just happen simply because a great period of time has passed. Great things happen because people do a great many things within a period of time before that time is lost.

How does one become more time conscious? One way is to set some goals. Another way is to simply give more attention to how you spend your day. Start the day with some kind of written document (I use 3 × 5 cards) which you've written which tells you what you would like to start, finish, investigate or achieve on that day. The things that don't get done that day will be put on tomorrow's card or appointment book. If you find yourself running your mouth about nothing, blowing time, just pull out your card to remind yourself what you had originally wanted to do that day. Many folks write a "Things To Do List" which is a good way of being time conscious. It forces you to at least list the things you know you should do. This list also should list the tasks in some kind of order to there is some sense of urgency to get at least some of them done. Since my purpose is to help you see how to make a better living for yourself, I would strongly advocate that you put at least one thing (besides going to work) that relates to money on your daily "things to do" list. If you are serious about building a fortune, you will include everyday some person, organization, institution, business, book, magazine or something which will add a piece of information on how to make your fortune.

I find, for instance, that most folks really waste their lunch hour. Lunch hour is for lunch, rest and is used to get a mental break from the grind or boredom of your job. But an ambitious person will use maybe 15-20 minutes to eat and the rest of the time to educate him or herself about how the money flows. Obviously if you work in a secluded or isolated facility you can't do this very well. But if you work at a down-town location you should visit banks and ask about credit or home mortgage rates, etc. Visit the library to see what new books came in on business. Visit the newsstands and look at the money management type of magazines. Lunch time should be job interview time. While other folks are sipping beer at lunch and complaining about their jobs, you're out there doing something about it.

As you progress in your time consciousness and money consciousness you will find that there is this great big obstacle standing in the way of your progress and keeping you from taking care of your business. The obstacle—your job. You see, the worse part about a job is that you spend all your intellectual, physical and emotional energy taking care of somebody else's business. When the day is done it's time for you to go home and give time and attention to your spouse, the kids, the community or members of the extended family. It doesn't even dawn on you that you've taken care of everybody's business that day (month, year) except your own. To me that is tragic because it means that everybody's business is more important than your own. A Fortune Builder cannot do this, and for a Black Fortune Builder it is disaster. If you are serious, your business is the most important business in the world. You can't do your business strictly on the lunch hour. Somehow your business must move from off stage to center stage. *Your* business must eventually be the thing you do from the time you get up in the morning to the time you put out the last light for bed. Two things cannot occupy the same place at the same time. Sooner or later the job has to go. Your real *job* is to build a fortune—period.

The ultimate sense of time consciousness is when you are not only giving all your time to taking care of your business but you have made it your business to figure out how to use other folks time to take care of your business as well. Is this exploitation? No. It's called job development and you know how the Black community is always talking about job development. Take care of your business, use other people's time and be a hero all at the same time, dig it?

THE BASICS OF HOME BUYING

Fortune Builders start out in most cases by owning the roof over their heads. Many people spend a great chunk of their life scraping to own the roof over their heads. That isn't necessary. The purpose of this section is to give you the absolute minimum bare bones information about what to expect when you seriously want to own your home. A separate chapter on real estate is included in this volume where more information and perspective can be obtained. Local conditions may mean significant differences with what you read here. There is no substitute for getting out there and finding out the situation for yourself.

When a piece of real estate changes hands, there are several parties who have to be satisfied or the deal will not be made.

a) The seller of the property has to be satisfied.

b) The seller's mortgage holder has to be satisfied.

c) The realtor or salesman representing the seller has to be satisfied.

d) The buyer has to be satisfied.

e) The buyer's mortgage holder has to be satisfied.

If the sale of a piece of property can be arranged in such a way that all five of these parties will walk away smiling and pleased, then you have yourself a sale.

Most home buyers do not know this very basic piece of information. They enter into the purchase of the most expensive and usually most important thing that they will ever purchase in their entire life . . . ignorant. I would like to explain what it takes in most cases to please these parties.

1. THE SELLER

The seller usually wants the highest possible price that he can get for his or her home. The home has been the largest single purchase that the seller has ever made (usually) and it has taken the largest amount of his monthly paycheck. The seller has spent many hours cleaning, repairing and caring for this building. For this tremendous financial and energy investment the owner wants top dollar. In addition to money and energy, the owner has something else invested in the property which he or she usually wants to be compensated for with money. That thing is emotion. People have an incredible amount of emotion tied to a house and somehow they think a buyer is to pay them for their emotional attachment with dollar bills. This can be a problem. Another thing owners want is the least amount of costs associated with selling the house. From the owner's point of view he has the asset, the thing which somebody else wants. Why should he or she have to pay a penny more than what they actually have in order to get his or her money for his or her house. If you can convince a seller that he is getting the highest possible price at the least expense *under the circumstances,* you will have a seller willing to sell.

2. THE SELLER'S MORTGAGE HOLDER

Few people pay cash for a house and those that can afford to usually don't do it anyway. This means that there is almost always some debt involved with most houses. If a person puts down $10,000 for a $50,000 house, he or she has a debt or mortgage of $40,000 that they owe to the mortgage holder. It was the mortgage holder who gave the seller the other $40,000 for the house. The mortgage holder is depending on the new buyer to pay this $40,000 back, plus interest, over a period of time (usually in years). When the new buyer decides to sell the house, the mortgage holder will want to make sure he gets the total balance owed him at the time the house changes hands. The mortgage holder many times has more money tied up in the property than the owner who is living in the house.

Example: One buyer puts down 10K on a 50K house. Over a period of time the house is now worth 60K and the buyer only owes $35,000 to the mortgage holder. The buyer has $25,000 of *equity* tied up in the house.

If the mortgage holder did not have to be satisfied, our buyer could become a seller and sell the house for $30,000. The buyer (who turned seller) would get all his $25,000 of equity in the form of cash dollars plus an extra $5,000 profit. The mortgage holder, however, would still need somebody to pay him his remaining $35,000 or he would have gotten screwed.

To summarize: When a property changes hands, the old mortgage holder has to be paid all his money from the new buyer before the actual owner gets any of his money at all. If the old mortgage holder is not satisfied (paid off), *there is no deal.*

3.   THE SALESMAN

The salesman sells houses for a living. He is an expert at knowing and doing all the right things to get a house bought and sold. The reason the buyer and the seller come to this salesman is because they both want to use him to get what they want. The buyer wants a house, the seller wants money. The salesman will help each party get what they want as long as he is paid. If the buyer and seller get what they want and he is not paid, then he is not satisfied and he will file a legal action to either prevent the deal from going through or to make sure he gets his money. What this basically means is that if a salesman is originally involved in the sale (they don't always have to be involved), then he has to get his money. Who pays the salesman his money? The seller pays the salesman from the big bundle of money he collects when the house is sold. The salesman's fee is part of the *cost* that sellers have to pay to get their house sold.

4.   THE BUYER

The buyer cannot be forced to buy a property that he or she does not like. This means that the buyer has to be satisfied or the deal doesn't even start, much less finish. The buyer buys a house for a million different reasons. Some of these reasons may include the location, size, nearby schools, the design, the cost, the neighbors, the land coming with the house or a multitude of other reasons. Whatever it takes to satisfy the buyer, he or she must be satisfied. Buyers have turned down houses because they didn't like one of the colors of the bathroom tile.

The buyer also looks to get the best buy that his or her dollars can possibly buy. The buyer stands opposed to the seller in a sense because where the seller is seeking the highest possible price for a house, the buyer is seeking the lowest possible price for the same house.

Buyers are also concerned with the terms they must agree to in order to buy the house. Terms can be a problem that stops the sale of a house even after the buyer and the seller have agreed on the price. Terms usually include a) how much of a downpayment must be given by the buyer to the seller; b) how much interest the buyer will pay on the mortgage; c) how long a period of time the buyer has to pay the mortgage off. The terms are basically set forth by the last and probably most important party—the buyer's mortgage holder.

5. THE BUYER'S MORTGAGE HOLDER

The buyer's mortgage holder is the key to any potential sale of property because it is the buyer's mortgage holder that provides most of the money in any deal. It is from the buyer's mortgage holder that the seller's mortgage holder gets his money and the seller his money. Sometimes even the salesman gets his money from this source. As in most situations in America and the world, the person, company or institution with the money gets to dictate what they want and how they want it. It is most important for people interested in buying a house to understand what their "backer" wants to see. They might then better prepare themselves when they apply for the purchase of their desired property.

A mortgage holder is usually a bank which means that we are dealing with a conservative lender. The bank is more interested in security and the soundness of the venture than obtaining high returns on risky ventures.

The security must be in both the property being bought and the lender asking for the mortgage loan. If either party is not just right, the bank will not make the loan.

The house must be of sound design and construction. The bank will send an inspector over to look at the house and the inspector will look for two things. The first thing he will look for is a sound house with proper working plumbing, heating and electrical units. He will see if the house needs repairs and recommend which repairs be completed before the final OK is given for the loan. The seller pays for the cost of any repair work that has to be done. This cuts down the seller's profit so they usually do all the essential repairs substantially before the house is put up for sale.

If the house is in good shape the inspector will then *appraise* the house which means make a determination on what he thinks the house is worth. This is a complicated process which need not be explained here.

Once the appraisal is made the bank can then tell you immediately how much money they will lend you for the purchase of the house. The money gap between what the seller wants and what the bank will lend is the gap that you have to fill and it is called the downpayment. If the price that the seller wants is greatly different from what the bank says the house is worth then there is a problem and somebody has to give in a little.

Example: A bank says they will lend 75% of the value of a house. John finds a house he likes and the owner says the house is selling for $100,000. John wants the house and hopes the bank will lend him $75,000 as a mortgage because he wants the house and he has $25,000 as a downpayment. The bank inspector comes in and says it's a really nice house but it is only worth $80,000 and they will only loan $60,000 (60K is 75% of 80K). This means that John has to either come up with another $15,000 to make a $40,000 downpayment or he has to talk the owner into coming down on the price. In actual practice, it is the salesman's job to convince the seller to come down in price. The seller can either come down in price or wait for another buyer.

If the problem of the price of the house is settled and the condition of the house is not a point of controversy, then the mortgage holder will look at the buyer. Usually what they will want to see is the following:

a) That the buyer's yearly income is at least half of the mortgage that the bank is granting. If the bank is lending a sixty thousand dollar mortgage, then the buyer's yearly income should be at least 30K per year.

b) That the mortgage payment is no more than about 30% of the buyer's monthly income (bring home pay).

c) That the total expenses going along with the cost of the house, such as taxes, insurance, fuel for heating and the utility bill (estimated) will be no more than about 40% of the buyer's take home monthly income.

d) That the total regular monthly debts *including* all housing expenses are not more than about 55-60% of your monthly income. In other words, banks want to see about 40% disposable income after all monthly bills and home payments. As you might be able to figure out on your fingers, these goals make it impossible for many folks to ever consider owning their own home. You can also see that if interest rates on home mortgages go up (causing the monthly payment to go up), people will be disqualified from from getting the mortgage (and therefore the house) that they want even though the house hasn't changed in price. If the fuel bill goes up, then people will lose also. If everything goes up at the same time, well, you should start to look at trailers to hook on the back of your car and not houses.

Actually, there are many, many ways to deal with these problems and it is a major reason for the writing of the book. These ideas will be discussed in the chapter on Real Estate.

THE BASICS OF TEAM DEVELOPMENT

When an employer is looking for particular kinds of workers, they interview maybe ten times the number of candidates before they make their selection. You must do the same when selecting your team members. Your team members are some of the most important people in your life. They will travel with you out of the jaws of poverty and powerlessness and ride with you to the other side of the spectrum where people do basically what they want to do because they can afford to. What are you looking for when searching for team members? That is a good question. Too often people just grab for the first lawyer, accountant or realtor that someone mentions to them. You do not want to do this. This is what you want:

1.   You want a team member who is honest but hungry. Just as you have made the decision to move ahead in life and put in the hours, the money and the worry it takes to do that, your team member should be likewise. What good would it do you if you've already made the decision to take some risks in life and your attorney constantly pushes you in the direction where the returns are poor because it's too predictable. On the other hand, you might have a sharp ambitious team member who is doing very well for himself or herself but is ripping you off to get there. Obviously, you don't want this either.

2.   You want team members who are accessible. Not only do they know you but their secretaries know you and when you call you get through to your man even though he's "holding all calls." Naturally there will be some situations where you guys miss each other, but that should definitely be the exception rather than the rule. Remember when you hire an accountant, an attorney, a carpenter, plumber or realtor, *they work for you.* I have seen situations where a person apologizes for "bothering" the very person he has hired to do his job. If your team member makes you feel like you are a drag on his time, get another person.

3.   You want a team member that teaches you things about his profession as time goes along. I strongly believe that a doctor, lawyer or insurance agent who takes the time to break down that strange language of their profession into ideas that you can understand, is a guy that is on your side. People who go off on a tangent in their secret terminology are usually more into head tripping and role playing than helping clients take care of business. Why shouldn't you know something about law after you have talked to a good lawyer for a few months? The more you

know, the better able you are to see if he or she is doing a good job. Many professionals don't try to explain things to you because they don't want you to be in a position to determine if they're doing a good job or not. These are the "Let me take care of everything" type of pros. Do you know how many people (especially Black athletes and entertainers, etc.) have been ripped off by the "Let me take care of everything" attorney?

4. You will want team members who are creative. As you progress in life you will realize that there are many, many ways to do anything. Sometimes it's to a person's advantage to do exactly what everybody else does. Other times it's advantageous to do the opposite of what everybody else does. And every once in a while it's good to at least try what *nobody* has ever done before. You will do well if you have a flexible, innovative, creative pro working on your side, who is not scared to try a different approach. To find these types of people may not be too hard because they will have reputations for doing things a little off base (but successfully).

Miles Davis, the continuously innovative Black "Jazz" trumpet player, would constantly surround himself by musicians young enough to be his sons to make sure that he wouldn't get locked into a sound that would reflect his true age. If you are forty-five years old, you may feel more comfortable with a professional your age. But it may be the young fella of 27 with 5 years experience that may have all the new creative answers you need. Check it out.

How do you find these professional team members who have all these good qualities? Well, I assure you; it ain't easy. You have to ask around and visit some of these characters and see if the "vibes" are good. Go to the nearest or biggest law school, business school, etc., in your area and talk to the Black upper-class students. (I assume you will want to try your own before moving to the "others.") Ask them, "Say, if I wanted to find a sharp business-minded brother that was heavy into law (accounting, tax, real estate, business, etc.), who would you suggest?" Ask maybe 10 or 15 students and the name that comes up the most often is the person you'll want to go see. If Black professionals are absent or found lacking (and it's crazy to assume that sharp Black pros are spread out evenly all across the United States), then ask the same questions to the White students and see who they come up with.

When all this searching and selecting is done, you have to have some project for these folks to eventually do. Otherwise you could be confused with the masses out there who just give all talk. I wish I could tell you that after careful screening, interviewing and socializing that you will be guaranteed satisfaction, but I can't. You won't know if your team members are any good until they are tested. But you won't even know then if you don't have enough fundamental understanding of what is suppose to happen in order to be in a position to judge their work. You see, some people get ripped off and find out. Others get ripped off and never find out. Dig it?

THE BASICS OF CREATIVITY

It might sound contradictory but the best way to be creative (if you don't feel you are naturally talented or creative) is to copy someone else's style. You see, a creative person has to have a beginning, a base, a starting point, and that can be found in a role model. After you spend hours, days or years copying the role model, you will find it impossible to continue. Somewhere along the line as you go through your daily maneuvers you will find a part of your brain or body insisting that a thing be done a certain way, a way that will be different from the role model. That, my friend, will be your own creativity coming through. At first it may happen only once in a while. But as time goes on, as confidence grows and as you respond more to situations that need immediate answers, your creativity will come through full force. Of course, this assumes that you do whatever your thing is everyday. Whether it's tennis, law, painting, music or studying the stock market, creativity comes from working from a solid base.

Another way to develop your creativity is to apply the ideas of one field to another field. For example, I'm sure that men's fashion is affected by women's fashion. American cars took on ideas of European cars, and it was called "creative."

Health spas have adopted some of the same principles that made McDonalds successful. In order to be creative in this way you have to have an awareness of what's going on around you other than you and your thing. That means reading, talking, listening and keeping up with what is happening in the world. If you find that you can't do that, I have one idea which may be helpful. Study t.v. commercials. Television commercials are perhaps the dumbest thing in the history of mankind. The thing which makes them serious is that they work. A lot of time and a lot of brains and money goes into studying how to program the public. If Bristol-Myers or Ford Motor Company decides to spend two hundred thousand dollars developing a minute commercial and then spends another two hundred thousand dollars to show the "dumb" commercial *one time* during the Super Bowl, you best believe that they've thought that thing out pretty good. All you need to do is study what they did. What little gimmick did they use? What style, color, sound, sex, speed, motion, fad or contraption did they stick in there to grab 15 seconds of your attention? Now, can that thing be applied to *your* thing? Think about it.

If I was at all successful, this section has given you a better idea of what concrete things you can or should do to get closer to your goal of the gold. The next section to follow, the Action Plan, is even more descriptive of what one person (me) thinks you need to do if you are serious about making drastic but positive changes in your life and life-style. The Action Plan is the heart of this book; therefore, the next section is important. Everything that I have described up to this very page is available for the most part in some other book of some sort. The Action Plan, however, is a little different because it not only tells what to do but more importantly why. Read it and think it over.

The Action Plan

The purpose of the Action Plan is to give the reader a chance to put ideas into a plan of action. Many people have a problem of not knowing where to start after they have been bombarded with a lot of information. This plan is designed to tell you how to start and why.

1. *SELF-ASSESSMENT.*

Self-assessment is really a continuous process, and I doubt that any person who takes their life seriously doesn't spend some time over the course of a year assessing where they are and how they got there. Self-assessment in this plan, however, is somewhat different because it is oriented towards money. It has to be if you are going to make any progress.

Look at your assets, your job, talents, your free time, your interests, goals and habits. Make a determination of just what you think you will need to feel happy and feel good about yourself. How much money per year *in today's money* do you think it will take to live *your* kind of life? Add 15% more to this year's cost to determine how much it will take to live that same kind of life next year provided there are no other changes, such as new children, sickness, fire, theft, etc. In order to do a really thorough assessment of yourself, you may have to ask some trusted friends and relatives what they think of your abilities, your job, personality, etc. This step is very difficult for most people to take, but it can be very enlightening. Weaknesses must be faced. If a person is fat, lazy, undisciplined, late, poorly groomed or has any other negative trait which is obviously holding them back, that point ought to be made clear by somebody.

The most important single question to be asked in the assessment area is, "How can I make more money?" I do not recommend illegal or immoral activities, but anything else you can consider should be considered. What have you succeeded in and failed in and why do you think you succeeded or failed? What would you really like to be doing 5, 10, 15 years from now if you could actually make it happen? What short term goals, say six months or a year from now, will you set for yourself?

117

These kinds of questions and a lot more have to be asked and answered by all who seek to improve their financial situation.

The end product of the self-assessment process should be a clearer idea of what you are going to do to make a better income both in the immediate future and the distant future. Hopefully, you will also decide about when you will be ready to leave your job and what enterprise of your own you will put in its place. The second result which should come from your self-assessment is simply (but importantly) the development of a *stronger determination to do* what you actually envision yourself doing.

2. *DOUBLE UP ON YOUR WORK EFFORTS.*

Thinking and assessing are important, but nothing really changes until the level of work and the product of work changes. It will be a requirement for quite a while for you to double the normal work effort you are probably use to. This means a minimum of 70 but more likely 80 hours of weekly work that you actually *get paid* for. This may be blowing your mind right now, but it is the most important single step of the whole plan because it makes so many of the other things possible. I will give an extensive explanation to convince you of the correctness of this step.

First of all, as Black folks we are often heard to say that Black folks have to work twice as hard and be twice as good to get the same credit or breaks as the White man. I believe this is often true. The problem with the phrase, however, is that people think that saying it is enough. Some folks must believe that if you say the phrase often enough, you will not have to actually do it. That, my friend, is not the case. You have to believe it *and* do it. You get no credit for merely saying it. The fact that it is said so often, however, means that many people already know an important part of what's needed to create change.

Secondly, you can look at an eighty hour work week this way. A hundred and fifty years ago our ancestors *had* to work 80 hours or more per week because they were slaves and it was either do that or be beaten, sold or shot. Their children, our great-grandparents, worked 80 hours a week because the life of poor farmers without machines or much manpower forced them to work those hours in order to scrape out a living out of the land. Their children, our grandparents and parents, had to work 80 hours or so because racism in the cities paid Black folks ridiculously different wages than White folks and they had more children and expenses to cover with their wages. Now we are here today in the 1980's with civil rights legislation and all kinds of college opportunities. We don't *have to* work 80 hours for the first time in over three hundred years to make ends meet. But we do have to work these hours to get rich, at least in the beginning. Now once you make your fortune your children and grandchildren will never have to even think of working 80 hour weeks. But they will be able to maintain the wealth that *you* will develop. If that is not enough motivation, close the book and pass it on to a person more serious than yourself. No hard feelings.

Thirdly, misery loves company. People can bear with hard work, sacrifice, problems and disappointment if they know other people are doing it too. Who else works 80 hour weeks. Let's see.

Doctors of all kinds work 80 hour weeks and are on call even when they are sleeping.

All those popular t.v. stars you love get up at daybreak and put on their makeup. When they finish reading their script, filming scenes and studying the next day's lines, the eleven o'clock news is over. A successful hour long t.v. series is not a fun thing to do.

Your congressmen in Washington have committee meetings to prepare them for more committee meetings. Breakfast is about politics, lunch and dinner is about politics, and evening drinks are about politics. When it is time to hit the campaign trail, the travel and handshaking and meetings could easily last 20 hours a day.

When Donna Summer or Earth, Wind & Fire or Parliament decide to go on tour, it works this way. The shows start at 8:00 p.m. and ends at midnight or later. Food, interviews and BS end about 4:00 a.m. They must then be up to catch a plane to Louisville at 8:00 a.m. They change planes in Louisville and get the plane to Houston after a three hour wait in the terminal. They arrive in Houston at 3:00 p.m. The sound check at the concert hall is at 4:00 p.m. They take a nap until the 8:00 p.m. show. Multiply that by a three-month tour and you can see the kind of dues they pay. James Brown (the hardest working man in show business) did over three hundred one-nighters a year during his heydays in the 1960's. In case you forgot, it's only 365 days in a year.

To sum it up, many, many people work 80 hours a week or more. The bar owner-bartender who serves you lunch at noon is washing glasses at 3:00 a.m. after he's closed up. The new McDonalds owner watches the girls serve you your Egg McMuffin at 7:00 a.m. and is still making french fries at midnight. A lot of people work 80 hours a week.
Benefits of the 80 Hour Week

There is a big difference between working long and hard at something you like and working it at something you hate. Money has no emotion. If you can understand the benefits of the 80 hour week, you might be better able to accept it.

More money stemming from two paychecks means:
a) Quicker payoff of bills. There is an indescribable kind of mental relief that one feels when the folks who bang our doors for money

owed them are no longer there. To pay off nagging bills that never seemed to go down before is like lifting a heavy weight off one's shoulders. This is a benefit of the 80 hour week.

b) A real savings account. I had said earlier that budgeting was important, but most Black folks living on the border of existence really can't be expected to put aside too much money from a single paycheck from a low-paying job. But by working a full time second job (or its equivalent in several part time jobs) is to create a situation where anybody can afford to put away one or two hundred dollars a month ($1,500-$2,500 per year).

c) A zooming credit rating. You have to understand that a bank credit manager is a human being and he can be influenced like the rest of us. When a decision is made to grant a person credit, a subjective decision is made directly or indirectly on that person's character as well as their income. When you can walk into a bank and prove that you work two full time jobs, you maximize both your income *and* character index. Credit should be yours for the asking so do a lot of asking. Keep applying for bank credit lines, credit union lines of credit and credit cards until you equal at least half of your total salary. That means a minimum of about $7,500 will be there one day when you need it.

d) A natural budgeting system. People spend money when they are bored. They buy things they don't really want or need and they know it precisely at the time they are buying it. But shopping and spending makes life a little more interesting. No wonder people have ridiculous bills. By working two jobs you will not have time or the inclination to create needless bills and so you have a budgeting system which is foolproof.

e) Nest egg development. In order to start any kind of business or investment program you need a savings nest egg or investment capital. With a regular savings plan, paid up bills and access to other money through credit, you can quickly (one or two years) get yourself in a position to make a substantial investment in a growing and promising venture. You couldn't do this by simply making ends meet from the one job.

f) Development of business hours. When Black businesses fail, a whole laundry list of valid and invalid reasons are given for failure. One of the reasons usually given is poor management which is such a vague term that it means everything and nothing at the same time. I think it is realistic to say that many folks want to do their own thing and run their own business but are unable to make a transition from the kind of hours an *employee* keeps (35-45) to the kind that *employers* keep (70 and more). In working two jobs one gets accustomed to the hours first without having to worry about the problems of getting paid. When starting your business, there should be a great increase in confidence when you know you can put the kind of time in that it takes in the early stages (the most crucial stages) of running a successful enterprise.

g) Being able to buy the roof over your head. The 80 hour per week worker should take maximum advantage of his high rate of disposable income (high income—low bills—good savings) to buy the best income-producing house he or she can find. The best type of house is probably a two or three family if you have a sizable family yourself or a four family if you can get by with smaller quarters. A talk with your realtor teammate and some shopping on your own part will help you make up your mind. If you are lucky, a good rent schedule may allow you to own the roof over your head for almost no money out of your own pocket. And you will have a tax shelter to protect you from the increased taxes from your two jobs. This would not have been possible with just one job.

h) The maximum use of time. Most non-professional folks or professional folks who find themselves working jobs get paid for the time they put in at the job and not for the quality of job that they do. By using 80 hours a week to be productive, rather than forty, you are making maximum use of your time in most cases. Using time well is habit forming. Once you get in the habit of using it, it feels very awkward and uncomfortable to resume wasting it.

The question could very well be asked, "Where are Black folks going to get these second jobs if there are not even enough *first* jobs to go around?" To that I would say that in spite of all the talk about their not being enough jobs, I continuously see many types of jobs advertised in the paper. America will have a difficult time running out of menial jobs for Black folks and Hispanic folks to do. It may seem crazy for a college educated young man to work for $3 or $4 an hour 'til one or two o'clock in the morning when he's making twice that amount or more in the daytime. But that is exactly what they should do if there is nothing left to pick from. Should a body who has struggled through school after waiting tables or being a barmaid for years go right back to that kind of work after they finally graduate? My answer is yes. The benefits explained above are too significant to blow on some ego trip behind the status of your new job or the concern with what your friends might say. I hope you can see it that way also.

I think you should also appreciate the cash flow advantages of working two jobs. You see, a person who works a 12K job and a 7K job will bring home more money than a person who works a 19K job. Why? Because at 19K you are taxed at a higher rate of tax than if you worked two lower paying jobs. The actual take home pay of a 12K and a 7K may be the same as a person making 21K or more. At income tax time you may have to make some of that tax up. But if you've bought your income property and learned about your deductions, you should have no problem whatsoever.

3. *SELF-EDUCATION.*

As part of the action plan there is a definite need to pursue all the kinds of information mentioned earlier that are necessary to the fortune building process. This would include information on home improvement and real estate development, tax deductions, savings and budget plans, etc. Most people would say this information is boring. Frankly, I find poverty boring. Actually, no information is boring if you intend to use it and actively look for ways to use it. The problem with most of us is that we have been through a school system where so few books and articles were of any practical use that we fear re-entering a ridiculous mind game which we thought ended when we received our diploma or degree. As I've said already, people do things out of habit; and once you learn the habit of reading for profit, you'll likely continue it for the rest of your life. If you do find some of these topics dry in the beginning, you have two choices to deal with the problem. One can either stick to interesting magazine articles where the material is short and sweet and varied or you can select biographies of business giants and get an insight into the events, mentality and methods that made them successful.

When does one do this reading if one is working eighty hours a week? Reading is like sex; if you want to do it, you will find the time. Actually, because of the low level of responsibility that America entrusts in the hands of the African-American, you may be able to do quite a bit of reading on the job. Secretaries aren't always typing, policeman aren't always patrolling, waitresses aren't always serving, and well, you get the picture. There is no race, no midterm test or grade to this kind of reading but you should digest at least some new idea or fact every week. Reading is very relaxing to some people so you may find yourself doing it at your off hours when nothing is on the television anyway. I have no doubt that once you see that there *is* actually information out there that will help you make and save money and work smarter, you will find the time to read with no problem.

4. *INVESTIGATE SALES.*

The most likely question that most readers may have at this point would be "How long does a new Fortune Builder have to work two jobs or 80 hours a week?" The answer to that question is that it will vary according to the interests, talents and circumstances of the individual. The important thing to remember is that the two-job routine is to serve a definition function, it is not to serve as a mere test of strength. You *are* to pay at least a good deal of your bills off, you are to improve your access to cash credit and you are to try to get an income-producing property to live in. If you don't do those kinds of things during this important period, then you're really wasting your time. A mere additional hundred and fifty bucks a week will not change your lifestyle. If you can accomplish all these things within 8-10 months—fine, but if it takes a couple of years, then keep the faith and do it.

Sooner or later, if you are serious, you will achieve the purposes which the eighty hour week is designed to meet. At that point it is important to take another important step which I believe more Black folks must and will do in the years ahead, investigate sales.

People in the United States (and the world for that matter) are paid according to their success in making an impact on the flow of money. A security guard, a school teacher, fireman or any other wage earner can only have so much effect on the flow of cash. As a result of that fact, they are paid a fixed income that remains the same pretty much the entire year. A salesman on the other hand is at the very center of the point where money changes hands. It is a salesperson's job to *make* money change hands and flow. Because success at this task is so important to different interests in this country, it is generally agreed that there should be some relationship between a person's ability to make money flow and their income. In other words, the greater ability to generate money flow the greater that person's earning capacity. Salesmen are the highest paid professionals in the country. Understand also that the term professional salesman is not just being applied to the guy with the briefcase ready to show you a brochure. Johnny Carson is both a commedian and salesman. Dr. J is both a basketball player and a salesman. Lola Falana is a dancer, singer and salesperson. Carson sells time on television, Dr. J sells $12 tickets to basketball games, and Ms. Falana sells admission and dinner tickets to night clubs. If you separate these stars' ability to sell from their actual talents, their bank accounts and assets would be no different from ours. It is their ability to generate the great changes in the flow of money that makes us even recognize their names and faces. There are people funnier than Carson and better at singing than Lola who are broke. It ain't about talent; it's about sales.

A Fortune Builder cannot remain ignorant to the world of sales. Everyone has the task of trying to figure out exactly what he or she is to sell in the world and learn about how to go about doing it as successfully as possible. Therefore, the next step, after working your two jobs and getting your financial life in at least minimum working order, is to

drop one of the jobs and spend time selling something. I think there is a
natural fear that most folks have, at least initially, regarding sales and
I think that this fear is even more pronounced among Black folks. But
there should be a difference in your attitude when you make the distinction
between the pressure of selling to put the food on the table and selling as
a second job after the main job has already put the food on the table.
There should also be a more willing attitude about sales when you understand the difference between taking any sales job because it's the only
thing available versus making the free choice of selling what you want to
sell.

It is very important for young (or old) Black folks to stop and take
the time to realize that in this country *anything* is for sale. All you have to
do is find something you like and ask yourself two questions: "Can I
make any money selling this thing?" and "How many other people could
I convince to like (and buy) what I like, to value what I value." All
three aspects or factors are absolutely essential for success in sales. You
have got to be clear about your own enthusiasm for the product, the
high potential for making a profit and the confidence that you can find
or convince people to buy what you both feel is an important item.
Without these three factors, no salesman can succeed. Fortune Builders
own their own businesses, and as a preliminary step to business ownership, experience with selling is a must.

It is assumed that a person eager to build a fortune will eventually
find a talent, item or some type of commodity to sell. At that point the
hours that use to go into the second job will now go into the sideline
selling activity. "Does that mean that we are back to 80 hours a week
again?" The answer is probably "no" for the simple reason that selling
is done at times and in places that are convenient to the consumer. Most
people limit their buying (except food and alcohol) to hours before
11:00 p.m. That means that one can expect to work a maximum of six
hours a night for the five week days. Saturday can be a good work day,
but the evenings are difficult; and of course most people are turned off
by Sunday selling. The purpose of selling as a sideline, however, is not
to match hour for hour but to increase productivity through increased
income.

Many a business person has started their ventures on a part time
basis and got their signal to go full time when their part time income ex-
ceeded their full time day job salary. If you grow to like both your selling
results and the lifestyle that goes along with it, then maybe you will
make your break with the job world and go full time also.

You may ask, "Why not start out selling part time rather than
working a menial job at a low rate of pay?" The answer to that is simple.
First, most sales can be rough in the beginning and the slow income
gains would make it difficult to pay off bills. Secondly, it is harder to

gain credit with a bank for either credit cards, credit lines or mortgages if your income is partly due to part time sales. Banks realize that sales is an unstable way to make a living and a part time effort means it's even a less dependable source of income. Sales income is a lot more difficult to check on than a salary at a job. All these reasons lead many banks to ignore the income coming in through part time sales and thus lower your chances of gaining the important credit rating that a second job would give you. Thirdly and very importantly, it takes more self-discipline to sell part time than it does to work another full time job. Most of us are job oriented. We go when we know we *have to* report and we work when we *know* there is going to be a paycheck at the end of the week. After we develop the habit of putting in the long hours we have the self-discipline to work our sales pitches and it's even easier since we know we won't be working as many hours. But to try to maintain a strict part time sales strategy in the face of early sales failures is a little too optimistic. Most of us just quit, go home and watch t.v.

During this period of investigating sales you have to not only look for a product that you feel comfortable in selling (and that's profitable) but you must also read and do some fact finding regarding the techniques of selling. Some people are natural salespersons while others are not. But everyone can benefit by additional study on the matter. There are sales expressions, philosophies, styles and techniques which can mean more money for the good students who take the time to learn and use them. The best part about learning techniques of sales is that you can use them not only in the sale of your product but in a hundred other situations as well. Any library or bookstore has many books with practical information and advice on this subject.

5. *DEVELOP A REAL ESTATE BASE.*

I'd like to describe a situation and ask you how you would react.

Your name is Fred and you hit the state lottery for ten grand which you quickly put in the bank. The next month you hand the teller your withdrawal slip and she says to you, "I'm sorry Fred, we no longer have your money." Your heart starts pumping and you yell out a long stream of curse words. The teller tells you to see the lending officer for an explanation. You go over to the lending officer steaming but you sit down. The officer comes over and says, "Fred, I'm sorry about your money; but you see Mr. Goodman came in here a few weeks ago with this dyna-mite business idea and he needed $50,000 to get it going. Your money was part of the fifty grand that we lent him to get his business going. Unfortunately, the deal fell through and we lost the money. You know how it is." Now what would your reaction most likely be?

(a) You're right Mr. Lending Officer, I know how it is. You guys

help get people started in business and you win some and lose
some. I'm sorry I lost my temper. I'll see you around.
(b) I don't give a hill of beans what you gave Mr. Goodman; I know
I put my money in this bank and I want my money. Your number one job is to safely protect depositors money, period. Everything else comes afterward. I want my money or I'm going to
raise a whole lot of hell around here, you can believe that.

If your response would be letter (a), I find you quite an unusual
person regardless of what color you are. I think I am on firm ground
when I say that most folks' reaction would be closer to letter (b).

The reason I make this point is because there is tremendous frustration on the part of ambitious Black folks who have been turned down
for business loans because they didn't have collateral. Collateral is those
assets which the borrower (of money) owns which is equal to or greater
in value than the actual money that is being borrowed. Thus, if I own
my house totally and it is worth fifty grand, then I may go to the bank
and borrow say forty grand using the house as collateral. The purpose of
collateral is to give the bank something to sell to get their money back
in case you die, stop making payments, etc. By using collateral as a
requirement for bank loans, banks always can be sure they are going
to get their money one way or another. What this means is that you
have to "be worth" at least what you are trying to borrow or the bank
won't lend it to you. Black folks and poor folks say, "You got to already
have the money before the banks will lend it to you," or "Banks will
only lend money to the rich; they won't lend a damn thing to the poor
man or the little guy to help him out." In many ways this is true. The
purpose of this book is not to be an apologist and capitalist supporter
of the banking establishment. Nor am I here to discredit or discuss the
methods of the neighborhood bank. I am simply trying to make a little
plainer and clearer how banks work and to relate some things that the
banking and educational establishments have failed to tell you. The
issue here is how do you get a "yes" from a bank after you've been told
no. Banks probably say "no" to requests of all kinds many more times
each day than they say "yes." To me that is not a problem. The problem
is that they never tell you how to get a "yes" from them.

The way you get a "yes" from a bank (in terms of a sizable loan)
is to develop a Real Estate Investment Portfolio. By that I mean you
must own several properties which are worth a great deal more than
what you actually owe on them. And this difference between what you
owe and what the true value is is called equity. When your equity is
about 1¼ to 1½ times the amount of money you want to borrow, you
should have little trouble borrowing your money. If the bank refuses the
loan for whatever reason, there are *second mortgage lenders* and *mortgage
brokers* who are listed in the newspaper and yellow pages who would be

happy to give you your needed business investment capital. How you develop this portfolio is the subject of the next chapter.

6. *ENTER A SUCCESSFUL BUSINESS ENTERPRISE.*

Successful business enterprise just does not happen, especially for Black folks, simply because you want it to. Success in business is a consequence, a result of many steps and factors which took place much earlier. One of the key factors which must take place is proper preparation on the part of the new business owner. White folks have successful businesses handed to them when they reach adulthood, but they already may have put in ten years or more of their time and effort learning the business during their adolescence. Black folks need a way to *learn* what is necessary and *have* what is necessary to successfully compete in business. The chapter on Business will discuss business and it will fill out the remaining portion of this plan.

7. *REPEAT ALL STEPS ABOVE.*

Even after you have started and reaped the benefits of your business, you will again access yourself. You will continually educate yourself because you will find that as soon as you have reached a certain level that it is not what you thought it was or there are some changes in the way the game is played (the way the business is run).

You will investigate new sales ideas and products. You will also continue developing your real estate portfolio because as a successful businessman you will continue to need tax shelter. Also, you will want to be in a position to borrow additional money anytime you need to.

Finally, as you grow in wealth, intellect, confidence, maturity and general ability, you will most likely find another perhaps very different business venture to get into.

Then you will repeat again most of the steps listed here.

SUMMARY OF ACTION PLAN

The Action Plan is designed to hurry through all the steps necessary for wealth and independence. A short summary here will go over the basics.

1. A determined Black person gets sick and tired of being poor and powerless and decides to do something about it. They spend days maybe months thinking, assessing, talking, reading and deciding exactly what they want and intend to do.

2. They take a second job working long hours saving the money that doesn't pay the essential living expenses and old bills.

3. They use the double income situation to improve on their credit standing and to buy a home that includes tenants to help pay the bills and provide tax deductions.

4. They begin to read and study magazines and books to gain useful information on business, real estate, taxes and sales.

5. They make the step of reading about sales to actually selling a product they find either important or exciting. They take their lumps and bruises, profits, losses and lessons along the way.

6. They take an active stand on real estate development and purchases and begin buying and improving a string of rented houses. They learn that their "net worth" or the value of their collateral will greatly determine what kind of business they can go into because it will determine how much they can borrow.

7. After the years of movement, learning, saving, investing and selling, they enter their chosen business knowing they are prepared and ready for success.

8. They repeat all the above processes in one form or another because they are ambitious, confident and prepared to do more than one thing at a time.

Special Notes to the Black Woman

I am well aware of the fact that all the information written in this particular section was written without any consideration of the responsibilities of parenthood. This was done because it is always much easier to address issues or answer problems when one is dealing with simple or normal situations rather than the abnormal or handicapped situations. It should be no shock or surprise to realize that in almost all cases it *is* easier for the single person or the married man with a wife at home taking care of the children to make the kinds of moves necessary to begin building a future fortune. Now that I have laid down the basic steps of what the "simple" situation would call for, I feel some responsibility to address the more difficult situation. In the Black community it is not abnormal for the single or separated Black woman to have one or more kids, be on welfare and knee deep in as much poverty and powerlessness as any person living in this country. As teenage unemployment and pregnancy and illiteracy all rise at the same time and among the same people, it is becoming distressingly normal. Another desparate group would include the ambitious Black woman who *is* married, but whose husband does not allow her to work and/or who cannot be motivated or expected to do any more than get by himself. Does she leave the kids and try to do it all herself and feel guilty about "breaking up a happy home" over money or does she hold on and go through her entire life at half or one-third speed wondering what *could be* if she were in a position to do her thing? These are heavy questions with even heavier answers. There comes a time when any person must acknowledge his or her limitation, and I for one will absolutely not offer any off-the-cuff marriage counseling here. I will, however, try to direct some of my opinions to the Black female parent who is already out there on her lonesome.

I think the first thing that Black female parents in poverty need to do is realize from the very beginning that their road is going to be longer, harder, riskier and will take longer to travel. That particular set of facts must be faced up to early. Otherwise you will find yourself setting yourself up for immediate disappointment and probably failure (failure = quitting the struggle). The facing up to this fact is not designed to give you a negative attitude, but simply to prepare you for the long haul and help you help yourself over those frustrating roadblocks to progress. You see, in track and field not only is the physical conditioning of the short distance and long distance runners different, but the mental preparation is greatly different also. As a single Black female parent you are automatically classified as a distance runner. You have a long race to run. Unfortunately, I have seen many, many Black women hurt by not facing up to this fact. They keep expecting that there is going to be one quick neat answer to all their problems and this quick answer is Prince Charming. They keep looking to marry themselves out of their situation. Price Charming, they think, is going to come riding by in a white Cadillac and lay a kiss on her lips, gold in her pocketbook and love all her children as his own. I won't say it's never going to happen. I'll say it ain't but so many Snow Whites and Cinderellas in the whole world. It's better to work like a man than look for one. Statistics say that even if you let all Black men out of jail and turned back all the ones that were "turned out" (you dig what I mean), that there still wouldn't be enough men to go all around for all you fine sisters out there. Watcha gonna do, be *poor* just because you're *lonely?* Maybe money can't buy everything (and then maybe it can?), but who said lonliness was better when you're poor too? My word of advice is to not wait for Prince Charming. Realize you have a lot of work to do and set it in your mind that nothing, maybe not even Prince Charming, is going to turn you around.

The second thing I recommend for the Black woman is unity. To me this is the *key* in gaining economic progress . . . unity. All oppressed or handicapped groups stick together; why not Black women? By unity I don't mean a unity against something (like Black men, for example) but a unity *for* something.

Let me give an example and raise questions at the same time.

Suppose two Black women, each with three kids, wanted to own their own house. If each is working a day job and selling some cosmetics on the side, why can't they apply for a mortgage *together* to buy a three family house? They can rent two floors and live together on the first floor. A year or two later they get themselves in a position to buy another three family house, again buying it together. They rent all three units and the house just about pays for itself. Now suppose for one reason or another they wanted to go their separate ways. What do they do? They go to an attorney and file two Quit Claim Deeds. A quit claim deed is just what it says. It means that the person named on the deed (a deed is a paper that proves you own a piece of property) quits or stops all claim of rights and ownership to the property thus leaving the remaining person as sole and complete owner of the property. Now if you have two families and two houses, each lady can file a quit claim deed to the other lady's house and they would each own outright a house that brings in income that they could never have owned by themselves. This is unity and it can get single Black women much further along the road than individual struggle. Unfortunately, just as it is difficult for Black folks to get together, it is probably even more difficult for Black women to work together. I am about to say some very subjective, opinionated things right here, but I'll tell you like I see it (and when you write your own book you can call it like *you* see it.) Black women get on each other's nerves. I don't know why, but I have met dozens of women who tell me that women are *petty*. Each sister probably meant a slightly different thing by her use of the word petty, but I'm assuming that they might have meant things like:

a) Black women keep and habor ill feelings for long periods of time after the misunderstanding is over and done with.

b) Black women are very jealous of each other's looks, men friends, children, intellect or any other of a million things.

c) Black women are so image conscious that life becomes much less a thing of developing substance than it does in developing the image which creates the illusion of substance. This could be why many White folks are confused with how well or how bad Black women are doing because all seem to dress like they are doing very well indeed.

I'm sure that White women have all the hang-ups that Black ones do. But we aren't dealing necessarily with the solution of White women's problems here. Besides, even if White women did have all these problems, it wouldn't help Black women solve theirs at all. It would probably make Black women accept the problems more and that would be horrible and backwards. (Black men's problems are very different, but a hell of a lot worse. They must be worse since they are doing almost all the killing, raping, arson, pocketbook snatching and drug dealing that goes on in our community.)

The issue and the point is that somehow Black women must learn to work together for economic ends. They must build their fortunes together regardless of personal differences or experience their independent poverty. In America everybody works together. The Mafia works together, the pimps and prostitutes and dope dealers work together, bank robbers work together. If the scum of the society can find partners and work together, why can't you find somebody to work with?

Your job is to go out into the world and find another female person (she may end up being White) to hook up with for business and financial development reasons—period. There is no escape from this responsibility as I see it for the great masses of single Black women.

The third thing to be dealt with is the care of the children. I have often heard doctors and mothers say that the first year of a child's life is the most crucial and the mother should be with the child as much as possible. I believe that. But I have also heard that first grade is the most crucial year and that sexual puberty is the most crucial year, that high school are the most crucial years, as well as everything in between. Let's face it; all the years of our children's lives are important. But in traveling the road to economic betterment, many sacrifices are called for, and time with our children is one of them. For the mother it is especially hard. But I believe it is even harder to be home with your kids and still be powerless to do much for them, to not provide for them and to not insure that their life will be any better than your own. I believe that the greatest thing that you can give a child is a shining example of a person who takes care of business. There will never be too many examples of people who take care of business in the Black community. Of course your children will be disappointed and of course they will not accept materialistic gifts and toys as a substitute for your love and attention. But as your child grows older and you become a better provider, he or she will understand what you did and why you had to do it. And as they in turn become adults and struggle with this world out here, your image of a serious-take-care-of-business woman will linger in their mind and serve as a guide when they get to their frustration points.

How does the mother arrange for the care of her children? This question is best answered by the reader. They know the day care centers, relatives, neighbors and friends whom they can trust and count on. If after all the looking you still come up empty, then you simply find a way to do productive work out of your home or apartment. Obviously, cutting down the work hours from 80 to 70 or 60 may help in the management of home life.

There are some of you who still may be convinced that all the benefits and sacrifices connected with long work hours may still not be worth spending the time away from your kids. You do have the right to disagree and you do have an alternative. You can sit home and play with your kids and collect welfare. But the cost of such an alternative may be great. For example, if a child sees his mother doing nothing but sit home and watch the t.v., what makes you think they will be motivated to do anything else? Why shouldn't they go into the under world and steal pocketbooks from senior citizens like everybody else on the block is doing? Why should your children even listen to you or respect what you say? After all, what do you know? All you've been doing over the years is sitting home watching t.v. and the real world is not t.v. Even if they do grow up strong and smart and are successful in life, they are still going to be frustrated. Why? Because if you're still alive and living in the ghetto, they are going to worry about you being the victim of somebody else's bullet, arson, robbery or other unfortunate circumstances. And if you are invited to their home to live, it will cause financial problems and arguments between the spouses. And if you're put in a rest or nursing home, there is worry, financial pressure and guilt associated with that. You see the problems of poverty and powerlessness follow you around until you're dead. It seems much better, at least to me, to spend two to seven or so difficult years and *get over the hump* and then everyone will benefit for the rest of the nearly fifty years that parents and children exist together here on earth.

Advantages of Being a Black Female Parent

Before you get too depressed about the problems and struggle of Black female parenthood, I think I need to let you know that there are many advantages that you can learn to work in your favor. You should know what these advantages are and make them take you to the top that much faster and/or easier. Let's check them out.

1. *DOUBLE MINORITY STATUS.*

During the 1960's Black folks struggled and protested to gain social, economic and political rights. During the 1970's women struggled and protested to gain the same things for women. The people who are going to gain all the benefits from these two decades of efforts will not be the ones home watching television but the ones who are pounding the doors of the offices filling out applications left and right and generally demanding to get a decent job. Fortunately, American corporations have adapted to the numbers game and especially like to hire Black women because they count in the statistics columns twice; once as Black and again as female. And who doesn't like to kill two birds with one stone (and one salary). Also, women no longer need to feel constrained to apply only for "female" jobs. A whole new range of employment opportunities are open that were never available before. Does this mean it's easy to get a job? No, it's never easy. But it's easier in some sense and I think that ought to be appreciated and taken advantage of.

2. *IN AMERICA, SEX SELLS.*

Sex has been used to sell probably every major item in America from alcohol and automobiles to vitamins and wristwatches. The face and body of the semi-nude White women has been offered to us as the reason why we should buy brand A shaving cream over brand X. There is one basic reason why this sexual suggestion in sales is used . . . it works, and when something works you stick with it. The Black female has an advantage, I believe, when it comes to sales. If the Black woman prepares herself to be presented in what the general society accepts as attractive (which may be very different than what *she* thinks is atractive), she will probably get the attention and ear of more potential buyers than a Black male would. Why? Because if she approaches a Black man to make a sell, the man will listen to the attractive female because his ego may tell him that he can make a successful "hit" here. He may even buy the product to impress the lady or hope that the sale will force a second meeting. The Black woman will listen to the sales pitch of another Black woman because she probably believes that if another Black woman is selling the product it should at least be worth a listen. In the Black community it is the men who have the image of con artists and sellers of cheap or stolen goods, not the women. What this means then is that many more Black women have the opportunity to make good money in sales than those that actually attempt to do so. The advantages of sales are many: flexible hours, independence and the chance for high pay with no chance of being fired. If you happen to be an attractive female, the sky is the limit.

A GOOD IMAGE WILL BRING MANY FOLLOWERS

When I look for the major differences between men and women, the words ego and competition keep coming up. I think women suffer some disadvantages from not having bigger egos and being less competitive, but I think they have some advantages in being less egotistical also. For instance, Black men really have problems following the leadership of other Black men. This is partially due to the fact that in a lot of people's minds the very idea of manhood means that you are *your own* man and therefore you follow *no* man. Women, I believe, will follow a successful trend, style or person with much less ego hangups than men. What does this mean for the single Black woman who wants to earn her fortune? It means she will probably have an easier time getting numbers of people (other women) to follow her in the development of a sales force than Black men would if they tried to do the same thing. We see the results of this all the time in church and day care fund raising activities and in home party sales shows. As a matter of fact, name any kind of community fund raising activity and a good majority of them were probably a group of women selling to other men and women. In fashion shows, cocktail sips, cosmetics, home care products or old fashion chicken dinners, the women were there taking care of business. An attractive, strong willed, organized Black woman who treats everyone fairly and doesn't get into the clique and "in-crowd" type of organizng can rather easily put a sales force together and make a mint.

MORE RESOURCES AT YOUR DISPOSAL

The majority of the women who pushed for female liberation the past ten years were White, and because they were White (and not quite as oppressed as they believed they were), they built organizations and institutions to assist women in need of advice and guidance. As a Black woman you may have reason to doubt if these organizations can serve your needs or not. The only way you will ever know for sure is to visit them and try to *make* them respond to your needs. Many White women want to believe that they are interested and can be of service to women of all races and income levels. Give them that chance so that you can benefit. If they have job contacts, free legal advice, and understanding of women's credit rights, etc., why not get all you can. At least the White women pretend to share ideas and services where the White man ain't giving up too much at all.

Deep down I believe that Black women have all the abilities and skills to do what is set forth in the book. As a matter of fact, it is my personal viewpoint that more Black women have the ability than the men do. What I find Black women lacking is enough role models to draw strength and encouragement from. This lack of role models has caused many talented Black women from developing the determination and the will to go all out and make a long sustained effort. Men with half the mental and artistic equipment go out so fired up that they get over anyway. If ever the importance of proper attitude held the key to future success, it couldn't be more so than in the case of the single Black female parent's struggle to make their financial waves in the world.

Developing a Real Estate Base

I think it is proper to begin this section with some hard cold facts about exactly what the situation is, as we enter the 1980's, regarding Black folks and real estate (land) in this country. The facts make a very tragic story, a very frustrating and a very scary story that is happening with mind blowing silence on the part of the Black leadership establishment of this country. It is a situation which, like cancer, will not be taken very seriously until it is much too late. The facts are this:

The freed slaves of the 1860's were supposed to get forty acres of land and a mule to work the land as a basis of self-support after the Civil War. Such land distributions were not made to Black folks for the most part due to many reasons that will not be discussed here. Nevertheless, by about 1915 or 1920 when the Black population numbered about half what it is today, Black folks owned about fifteen million (15,000,000) acres of land in these United States. Twelve million people concentrated primarily in the Southern part of the U.S. owned more than one acre of land for every man, woman and child in the "Nation within a Nation."

Beginning after World War I, again for reasons that will not be discussed here, Black folks began to lose their grip and their ownership of this land. Many Black folks quite honestly walked away from the land and came North to seek a better life. What started out as a trickle became an ocean wave. Thousands of us Black folks moved North leaving behind many problems and frustrations including that old handkerchief head cotton picker image that embarrassed many sensitive Black folks. What should have happened under an ideal situation was for the *location of Black-owned land* to change with the actual change in location of the people. But what actually happened was that in exchange for land ownership, Black folks aspired toward and settled for a "fancy apartment." Most Blacks didn't get a "fancy" apartment, just an apartment. Segregation patterns of Northern cities put them in the oldest, most run-down and crowded sections of town. The trade-offs or benefits that

136

Blacks were looking for in addition to the "fancy apartment" were better schools, health care, job opportunities, etc. What many Blacks got was a concrete box stacked on top of twelve other concrete boxes called "projects," and the job opportunities and all the other goodies just never came in enough abundance to satisfy the masses of folks.

Today in 1980 we are at least twenty-five million strong as a people. But folks, we own only *six* million acres of land. With more than twice the population we own less than half as much of America as we did just out of slavery. Even if Black folks began a "Buy Property Movement" and *doubled* Black land ownership in the next twenty years (a highly unlikely occurrence for many reasons), we would still enter the twenty-first century with less than half the land for every man, woman and child that we had back in World War I years. The fact is, however, that there is nothing even close to a Buy Property Movement among Black folks. On the contrary, Blacks are being turned out, pushed out, taxed out and frozen out of their properties in the Northern sections of the country while still losing about *ten thousand acres a week of land* in the Southern part of the nation. As I have said before, the forces of nature and White folks keep changing the rules of the game for Blacks and the frustration is unbearable. When Blacks lived in the South, the North was the "promise land." By the time half the nation's Black folks moved North, we were told of shrinking city budgets and services in the "Frost Belt." The promise land today is the "Sun Belt." Where is the Sun Belt? It's California and Arizona, but it's also Texas, Louisiana, Mississippi and Alabama too. All Black folks old backyards are in today's "Sun Belt." For better or for worse, the trend of Black folks moving back down South is already a half dozen years old or more.

For the Northern ghetto child, their chances of land ownership is virtually nil because every part of owning a home is going up every year. By the time you add taxes, heating costs, interest rates and repair costs on top of steadily rising home prices, you can easily see the handwriting on the wall. The hard cold fact is that due to the factors above and especially due to the fact that no public educational systems give adequate instruction on how to purchase property and repair homes, most Black folks will own, occupy and control more square footage of ground when dead and buried in their grave than they will while they are alive. If that doesn't sound tragic or frightening to you, then you can see why we still have the problem.

Perhaps it should be made a little clearer why Black land ownership is important. Black folks are the largest minority group in America. As all the other segments of the American population vie for power and influence, each group seeks to maintain and develop their power base in order to maintain their power. Some interests in this country own and control the oil supplies; that is their power base, and the politics of the federal and state governments reflect the influence this power base quite often. Other interests control the grain and agricultural supplies and other groups dominate the professions, manufacturing, the press or even the underworld. Now what is the power base of Black folks? It use to be that we were the labor supply which had the greatest impact on the agricultural growth of the nation when the agricultural sector of the economy was the most important. But we weren't in *control* actually because we were slaves and slavery controlled us.

But the land that Black folks owned *after slavery,* those fifteen million acres of land was and could have still been a solid base of Black power and influence had it remained intact. But the statistics now say that losing control of 10,000 acres of land a week will leave Black folks virtually *land less* by the beginning of the year 2000 which is only a short twenty years away. That would mean that Black folks would own virtually nothing of value and control nothing of value. History shows that people who do not own a piece of their neighborhood, who don't really have roots or a stake in the neighborhood, simply do not vote. Thus the land ownership question is tied to control of local politics and thus affects another major source of power and influence. To make all these matters worse, it is at this particular time in Black and American history that urban school systems produce students that read *worse* than many of the escaped slaves. Many of today's students have less interest in reading and writing than the slave who could have been *killed* for learning such skills (but who pursued them anyway!).

What can you or I do as individuals to help turn these chain of events around? I wish I knew a simple answer. The only thing that seems to make sense to me is for the concerned Fortune Builder to be a shining example for the people. Once you escape poverty and powerlessness you light the way for a few others to do the same thing. When the forest is dark at night you don't expect the sun to come up, but you would like to have a light. One light can light up enough of the forest for you to find your way. In the Black community we need lights. We need people to prove to the masses that you don't need to be super talented in athletics and music or super intelligent in science and math to escape poverty and powerlessness. The more Fortune Builders the Black community produces, the more young folks will see the relationship between work and wealth and between study and wealth. Right now the only people talking about work and study are parents, teachers and preachers. They never mention money in their conversation, and they don't seem to be doing too well themselves. If Fortune Builders don't make their presence felt within the decade of the 80's, then maybe all the old concepts of work, sacrifice and learning will be lost and Black folks will fall further back in time and relevance in the real world.

Let us now see how even with all the previously mentioned problems, real estate is still the key to earning wealth.

THE PURPOSES OF REAL ESTATE INVESTMENT

I think it should be made clear now, if you have not heard it before, how important real estate investment is to fortune building. The facts are that more people have become millionaires and multi-millionaires through investment in real estate than all the other methods of making money *combined*. It's that heavy.

When stockbrokers make gains in the stock market, they invest in real estate. When the actor makes a fortune in the movies, he buys real estate. When the All-Star athlete signs the big contract, his legal representatives advise real estate purchases. The institutions like colleges, insurance companies, banks and all major corporations all invest in real estate. There are many reasons for this.

First of all, real estate is plentiful. The whole damn planet is one big piece of real estate, at least the two-fifths that we call land is anyway. From the time you open your eyes in the morning to the time you close them in the evening and including the sleeping time in between, you are walking, sitting, riding over or lying down on somebody's piece of real estate. Somebody is making money on virtually every house, store, office building, sports arena, apartment complex, shopping center or car wash that you see. So the fact of land's plentifulness is one reason why almost everybody has some future goal of owning real estate.

Secondly, real estate has almost unlimited uses. Some people grow food on it, others dig for gold and silver or drill for oil, while still others raise cattle or put up office buildings. In short, whatever you can use land for is what you can invest in real estate for. It's the same thing.

Thirdly, the extreme permanence of real estate makes it the absolutely safest thing to invest in. Land is not going to be killed, swiped or kidnapped, nor will it break. Land and buildings were here before you came and will be here after you leave. In Viet Nam, some pieces of ground were bombed sixty or seventy times. It may be years before the area grows normal vegetation, but the land is still there. Any person, no matter how conservative or cautious, can make a real estate investment and be virtually certain that they will not lose what they paid for.

Fourthly, real estate almost always goes up in value. There are entire courses on land use and value, so I will not try to explain such principles here. But given certain basic conditions, land and buildings generally increase in value over the course of years. Investments by nature are supposed to increase in value over time so land and real estate are perfect investment tools.

Finally, and most importantly to many real estate investors, real estate can create fabulous amounts of monthly cash income without the investor having to do any work whatsoever.

You would think perhaps that with real estate being such a good thing, such a "sure" thing, that anybody and everybody would put their money up and be happy ever after. But real estate can be very complex, very expensive and even very risky if you don't know what you are doing. In this little section I will try to lay out in rather simple language the basic purposes of real estate investment. At the end of this volume you will find books which are much more complete in their explanation of real estate ideas and principles.

PURPOSE NUMBER 1—TAX SHELTER

A tax shelter is very much what it sounds like. It is a device, an investment device, which helps the investor pay less of his income out to the government in the form of tax money than he or she would pay without the tax shelter. Black folks generally aren't educated or involved in tax shelters because due to their low incomes, they don't pay much money in the form of income taxes anyway. But many single persons earning say 22K or more a year or a couple earning say 30K or more a year should seriously begin to look for a way to save some of the money they are paying the government in taxes.

How does real estate help you save taxes? To understand that idea you have to first understand what interest, repairs, expenses, taxes and depreciation are and how they figure into the overall formula. Interest costs are that portion of mortgage payments which the lender can keep for himself as profit for lending you the money. It is that part of the loan which you pay in addition to the actual amount of money that you borrowed. In real estate investments it is quite common for a property to cost actually three times the stated cost because of all the interest costs. If for example a 25K house is to be paid off in 25 years at a 10% interest rate, you will find that your 25 year total of payments will be around 75K or more. Interest rates are deductible from your income when tax filing time comes around. Repairs are quite simple to understand. When something in an investment piece of property breaks down, you repair it. The costs of these repairs are deductible from your income also. Expenses are also quite simple. Anything that is a regular cost to running your real estate "business" from heating and electricity to snow removal and trash removal is an expense which is deductible from your taxable income. Taxes are real estate taxes which every owner of real estate must pay to the town the property is located in to help pay for the school systems, library system, trash pick up and all other city and county services. Taxes are deductible.

Depreciation is an idea which may be a little strange to understand but is really very simple. When you build a building, that building is given a lifetime of a certain number of years of what is called "useful life." It means that the federal government is accepting the fact that buildings don't last forever and like a car they can be expected to be useless over a reasonable period of time, usually 20, 25 or 30 years. If you divide the cost of the building by 20, 25 or 30, you will arrive at the yearly depreciation amount which you can say you "lost" in value of your asset. In truth you haven't lost anything, but "on paper" you lose one useful year of your building every time a year passes. Now let's look at some numbers.

Sam Spade makes 40K a year as a cook. Sam is single and must pay the government 12K a year in taxes because he doesn't have any expenses or deductions. In order to pay the government less taxes you must show "on paper" that you really aren't making as much profit or income as it looks like you are making because of the other expenses you must pay. After you subtract your costs you are left with your "real" profit or income which will be a much lower figure. Because it is a lower figure you will pay lower taxes. Sam buys an apartment house with 16 apartments in it; but he has a management company do all the collecting, buying, bill paying and everything that needs to be done because all he wants to do is cook. The building costs 200K and the taxes are 12K a year. The building collects total rents of 41K for the entire year. Let's look at the results.

Sam Spade Income 1980

Salary	40K	
Rents	41K	
	———	
Total Income	81K	
Expenses		
Taxes	12K	
Utilities & Heating	5K	
Mortage & Interest	20K	
Repairs	2K	
Other Expenses	1K	
Management Costs	1K	
Depreciation	8K	(200K divided by 25 years)
	———	
Total Deductions	49K	

Total Income 81K — Total Deductions 49K = 32K

Tax to be paid on 32K = 7K income tax

In the example above, Sam did not make any cash money in his hand from the rents, but he knew that ahead of time before he bought the apartment building. He bought this particular building for tax shelter purposes, not income purposes. What Sam did do is reduce his taxable

income from 40K a year to 32K a year. Because the tax rate between
32K and 40K is very high, Sam saved 5K in taxes paid to the government. He will get a 5K check back from Uncle Sam after he files his
taxes and he didn't have to do any work because the management company took care of everything. In this example Sam "sheltered" 8K of his
income, but it was the most important 8K because it was the top 8K which
is the amount taxed at the highest rate. But this is not all Sam got out
the deal! Some of the rent money paid down the mortgage, so instead of
owing 200K for the building in 1981, he will only owe 198K. He has
2K in *equity*. But there is more good news. Sam's building increased in
value 10% in 1980, so it is now worth 20K more or 220K. If you add
up all of Sam's benefits in the one year, you have:

> 5K in tax money refunded
>
> 2K in mortgage payment "equity"
>
> 20K in increased value
>
> ———
>
> 27K in total benefits

Can you begin to see the value of real estate?

PURPOSE NUMBER 2—APPRECIATION

There are some people who are not concerned with tax shelter because
they have other ways of protecting their income. What these people are
looking for is a way to have their money work for them by giving them
a higher return than banks and a greater chance of a return than the
stock market. Real estate accomplishes this by a principle called leverage.
Leverage is used when you take a small amount of money to buy a large
or valuable building and that building is still gaining in value. Rather
than calculating the growth of your small downpayment, you calculate
the growth on the value of the whole building.

In the example of Sam Spade above, let us assume that Sam had to
put down 20K as a downpayment on the building that originally cost
200K. If the building increases in value 10%, that 10% is applied to the
whole value of the building and thus is a gain of 20K (10% of 200K is
20K), not just the amount of Sam's money where it would have only
netted him a gain of 2K (10% of 20K is 2K). Now a bank pays 5% or
7% or 12% in interest on money you save with them. Compare the
return Sam gained in real estate with the gain of the banks. Twelve percent of 20K equals $2,400 (2.4K) as compared with 20K gain in value.
What percentage of gain did Sam make on his money in the real estate
deal?

200K building — 20K downpayment = 180K balance.

An increase of 10% = 220K building — 180K balance.

220K — 180K = 40K in Equity.

If Sam's 20K investment (equity) went to 40K (in equity) in one year, then his investment is doubled. When your investment doubles it means you got a 100% return not just 12%. Can you begin to see how real estate fortunes are made?

PURPOSE NUMBER 3—RENTAL INCOME

Suppose Sam decides to stop cooking after twenty-five years and he still has his building and it's in pretty good shape. To make matters simple, let's say that everything doubled in that time, the rents, expenses, repairs, heat, everything. One thing would be missing however, the mortgage payment, because the place would be paid off. How much money would Sam make from his building?

Double rents would mean 82K coming in. Double taxes, heat, repairs, expenses, management = 42K going out. Leftover for Sam to spend for doing no work is 40K a year. If Sam decides to sell his place he will get 400K minus selling expenses and taxes. Even if Sam was left with only 300K, wouldn't that be a pretty good sum? Now answer two questions: 1) What work did Sam have to do? Very little; the management company did the work. 2) How much money did Sam have to put out to get this 300K? Only his 20K downpayment; the tenants paid off the rest with their rent payments. I repeat—20K leads to 300K with no additional out-of-pocket money.

Now can you see how real estate fortunes are made?

Suppose Sam saved the same 5K in taxes for 25 years. That would be 125K more in profit for a total of 425K in his hand for a measly 20K downpayment.

In reality many deals don't work out as well as this one. But if you can believe it, many work out *much* better. I also do not want to give the impression that buildings have to be paid off before one can make rental income. *Most* buildings are sold for rental income purposes because rents *do* amount to more than expenses and a profit is made from the first year onward. I hope all this information will encourage you to study the books on real estate listed in the back of this book.

Perhaps the following chart can show you in stronger terms the value of sound real estate investment. Looking at the growth in the value of one's original nest egg (and not even dealing with cash, return income or tax shelter benefits which would obviously increase the percentage of one's return), compare the following five year results of persons A, B and C who have 50K to invest.

"A" deposits 50K in bank and earns 12% interest compounded yearly.

Start	50.0K
After 1st year	56.0K
After 2nd year	62.7K
After 3rd year	70.2K
After 4th year	78.6K
After 5th year	88.0K

A gain of 38K over 5 years.

"B" invests in stocks or bonds bringing in 15% compounded yearly.

	50.0K
	57.5K
	66.1K
	76.0K
	87.4K
	100.5K

A gain of 50.5K over 5 years.

"C" makes 20% downpayment in a building that gains 10% a year.

50.0K	Building Value 250K
275.0K	Building Value
302.5K	Value
332.7K	Value
365.9K	Value
402.5K	Value—Old Mortgage of 200K

A gain of 152.5K over 5 years.

Although the percentage of return on the building is lower than that of the bank and the stocks, the growth in value of your investment is three times greater. This is because the growth in the bank deposit and the stock is growth strictly on the exact amount of money that you put in. In the building situation, you have the whole value of the building growing for you of which you only had to put down a partial downpayment of 20%. Remember, also, that I said this comparison does *not* include the tax shelter, rental income or mortgage pay down aspects of the real estate investment. Now can you see how real estate fortunes are made?

UNDERSTANDING THE DIFFERENT RULES FOR
THE SAME GAME

In the previous chapter I tried to make clear two ideas which related to real estate and business. The first was the brief discussion on what was basically necessary to purchase a home. The second was the idea of developing a real estate base for borrowing money where the real estate can be used as collateral. These two ideas will be expanded upon in this section.

Let us assume for the sake of argument that you have gotten the basic aspects of your financial situation together. You are working a decent job and you are selling something on the side, putting in the hours and saving your money as best you can. We will also assume that your bills are paid down, you own a three family house and your credit is in good shape. After a lot of reading and questioning of other business-men, you have identified the business you want to go into. It is a business that is ripe for both your interest and personality as well as being highly profitable. After talking to your lawyer, banker and other team members, you determine that you need 50K of your own money to get the ball rolling for your business. Where do you and how do you, as a working man, amass $50,000 of your own money (before you get too old to even walk)? That is the basic question that has stopped many an ambi-tious, optimistic entrepreneur dead in their tracks.

I believe the answer is in building a real estate base. You must amass *more than* 50K in equity value in property which you own to then be able to borrow the 50K and start your business.

For White folks this idea is fairly easy. They simply begin to buy property in *their neighborhood,* improve it, and in no time at all they have the needed equity to go get their loan. For Black folks the case is much different. Why? Because of a very, very real situation that every-body knows but few really come out and say.

Property in the United States of America has its value determined in direct relation to how close that property is located to Black folks— period.

In city after city it is easy to find two houses of equal quality which have very, very different price tags. The lower price tag belongs to the house of the Black family and the higher priced house belongs to the White family. You can read over fifty real estate books (as I have) and you will never see the ideas that I am about to lay on you right now. However, to be Black and not be aware of these ideas is to set yourself up for big disappointments.

a) When people buy a house, they don't just buy a house; they buy *a whole neighborhood.* Most adults are interested in the school system, the crime statistics, the police and fire response to problems, the nearness and quality of the hospital, the garbage pickup, and most certainly the *taxes* as well as a multitude of other minor features.

When all of these neighborhood features are excellent and show every prospect of remaining excellent, not only will the same house cost a lot more, the very *ground* that the house occupies may cost, by itself, as much as the whole house would cost in a more rundown area. This is because people don't live in just houses; they live in communities and communities are much harder to build than houses.

b) When people buy "good neighborhoods" they can be *sure* that their house (the largest investment they will ever make in their life) will go up in value. There will be no need for hoping or guessing on this point.

c) Black folks for sociological reasons (which this book will not get into) are found guilty of both petty and serious crimes more often than Whites and thus are associated with crime itself. Black folks do suffer more from unemployment, learning difficulties, poor health and other problems which in total do effect local tax rates, school, etc. Thus, Black folks are associated with all the problems that the person who buys a home is seeking to get away from.

d) It is a pretty well-known theory that better than 90% of all pranks and acts of vandalism are committed by pre-adolescent and teenage youngsters. Black folks generally have more children per family. The more kids, the more possibility of vandalism and property destruction. Thus in the minds of White folks, Black families in the neighborhood mean greater chances for vandalism and property destruction.

e) Black folks on the whole would rather live around at least *some* additional Black families rather than live in racial isolation. Thus, Black families are quite likely to follow other Black families to the nicer neighborhoods. This is no different for the most part than any other ethnic group seeking to feel a sense of community (in terms of similarities and values) in their neighborhood. Thus to White folks, one Black family guarantees that there will soon be more.

f) Most Black folks utilize the low downpayment government programs for home purchases. This often means that they do not have a lot of money invested in their property and may be less inclined to keep up their asset (their home) which does not represent a significant risk of their money. Many Black folks (and White folks also) have a greater downpayment in their car than in their house and keep up the maintenance of their car better than they do their house. There may be very sound reasons why this has to be the case. But to people who buy a home as an investment which is to gain in value, all the explanations and reasoning mean nothing.

g) White folks realize that each and every problem they are seeking to get away from could very well be brought into their neighborhood by other White folks. However, statistics and objective facts relating to racism and poverty make it seem *more certain* that those problems will happen if Black folks are neighbors.

Thus, the bottom line across America is generally avoid the Blacks if you want your house to gain in value. There is one other factor which causes great changes in value of property and that is the factor of supply and demand which I will try to explain as best as I can.

Demand really means *desire*. When something is in demand it means there are large numbers of people desiring that particular thing. Now suppose Black folks moved into a neighborhood and there was absolutely no change in the school system, tax rates, crime, etc. However, let's say everytime a person did decide to move according to a natural progression, it was a Black family that moved into the newly sold house. What this would mean is that there was no great demand or desire on the part of the majority of the buyers (White folks are still the vast majority of Americans and are so even in *most* cities) or White folks to move into that neighborhood regardless of its stability. When there is no great desire on the part of the majority buyers of anything, the price cannot go up but so high. There would be a great desire on the part of the minority buyers for a house in this neighborhood because it has all the things that Black buyers are looking for: stability and familiar neighbors. But most Black buyers use federal government buying plans and there is a limit as to how much these programs will help finance on a house. These government housing cost limits almost are always below the cost of new houses in middle class neighborhoods or the more desirable middle income sections of town. Thus, *who wants* the house and *how* the house is going to be paid for will greatly determine how high the houses are likely to climb in value.

It is important to understand that there are various exceptions to the rule on race and housing value. One factor is the price of the house. If a Black doctor making 100K a year buys a house at 250K, his house is in no danger of losing value. The cost alone will keep almost all other Blacks in that particular town out of that neighborhood where the surrounding houses will cost just as much or more. The Black doctor has to deal with two situations. The first is how does he and his family feel living in an all White neighborhood? Do they feel they live in a warm community or do they find themselves relating only to their house and its grounds? Secondly, how does the White neighborhood treat their new Black neighbor? Do they respect him as a man of success with talent comparable with their own or do they burn crosses on his or her front lawn because they hate Niggras anyway?

A second exception is when a neighborhood is so well known to the nation as a prestigious area that anybody could move there and wouldn't have to worry about falling housing values. These places might be Beverly Hills, Bel Air and Marin County in California, Greenwich in Connecticut, or certain Westchester County or Long Island communities in New York.

A third exception and the one most obvious to Black folks today is the Gentrification Movement in the cities. Gentrification is a term used to mean that certain young, talented, somewhat wealthy White folks are reclaiming parts of the Black community because it lies close to an important institution, facility or neighborhood. The Haight section of San Francisco, the Society Hill section of Philadelphia, and various parts of Washington and Chicago are seeing Whites come in, Blacks going out and property values going to the sky. This is due to the fact that demand (the desire of White folks to have such property) is creating higher prices. Not only are the houses being completely renovated and modernized and neighborhood shops taking on a different flavor, but a new community of artists, professionals and scholars is being developed at the same time. It is the desire on the part of the large segment of White folks to be a part of this "in crowd" that is being newly formed that adds greatly to the new value of old Black folks' old homes. The Black folks must go so that the numbers and kinds of people that is to give the area its new value can come in.

All this information has been laid out so that it will be obvious that Black folks generally can't go out into the world and expect to play the real estate game exactly the way White folks do and expect to walk away with the same benefits. But I don't mean to imply that you can *never* play it the way White folks do either. The secret is in knowing when you can and when you can't. That knowledge comes only through first-hand experience and study. It cannot be taught completely out of a book.

BLACK FOLKS' ANSWER TO RACISM IN REAL ESTATE

MAKING SOMETHING OUT OF NOTHING

In the previous section I painted a very negative picture with regard to Black folks, land and housing values. Actually, I would use the word truthful rather than negative because I seek to be truthful more than I seek to be negative. In this section I hope to show that all is not lost, that Black folks can build a significant net worth in real estate equity value as long as they know what to do, how to do it, when and where to do it.

As a general rule I'd like to say that Black folks gain their values through wholesale buying, conversions and improvements rather than simple appreciations. White folks in many instances don't have to do anything but maintain their houses as they are and over time the houses will automatically rise in value. In Beverly Hills it is not at all uncommon today for a person's house to increase in value by a half a million dollars in say three or four years, while they may not have done anything but paint the place and cut the grass. Black folks must *add value* to their properties by creating new uses and renovating important areas. The purpose of this section is to lay down the basics so that you can then consult four or five real estate books with a better understanding of how to apply the valuable information that you will find in them.

The way to real estate wealth in the Black community is to create something out of nothing. Every major city in the U.S. has neighborhoods where there is bad housing, housing so bad in fact as to be classified as almost worthless. The phrase that is popularly used is "unfit for human habitation." Now in some areas where virtually every house or every other house looks this bad, the thing to do perhaps is to pass the whole area up. Of course this depends on a multitude of factors. Nobody should pretend, however, that they can singlehandedly take on a whole community and restore it to its former state. If, however, you find a rundown house in a basically stable area of town, you need to do some research to see if you have a potential gold mine. In order to "create value" or "add value" to a piece of property, you have to do many things and learn many skills. I have developed the following list so that you can get an idea of what is necessary to create something out of nothing as it is much more complex than simply improving rundown houses. It will take time, especially if you are working by yourself, to learn all these skills and situations; but I assure you it will be well worth your while when you can understand and apply them. Your teammates, the realtor, banker and attorney, can be of great assistance in explaining details after you have studied enough on your own to get the broad picture.

1.   LEARNING HOUSING VALUES

The first step in your real estate strategy is to learn the general value of the houses located in the areas that interest you. This is important for two reasons. The first reason is that you must see what people generally are willing to pay for the houses in your area as that will probably be the value of any house you are likely to own in that area also. One extremely important rule to understand in real estate is that a property is worth what you can get for it and only that amount, period. You see, when you go to a bank to get an estimated value of your car or the car you want to buy, the banker pulls out a blue book and says, "Your car is worth x number of dollars." How does he know? Because the car company that made your car made 200,000 just like it and they are selling all over the country for a certain price give or take a hundred dollars and depending on condition. But every house in America is unique. It is located at a certain spot near certain other houses, people, places and things and none of that can easily be changed. The house is worth what the three or five couples that are looking at it tell you that they can or will give you for it. You either accept one of their offers or you hold onto your house. It's that simple.

The way you find what the housing values are in your area is to visit a local real estate office and ask to see the book on recent purchases of local property. In this book you will actually see pretty much what people paid what price for each listed property within the last couple of months or so. You go by these properties and after seeing at least the outside of a few dozen houses, you will be able to approximate within a few thousand (or less) dollars the probable selling price of a house. You can also check current house listings and visit houses as if you were shopping for one yourself. Between the two methods you will develop an ability to guess the value of each house that strikes your attention.

The second reason to learn housing values is to be able to recognize a bargain when you see one. A bargain is a house that is priced below the general market rate or the "fair market value" or lower than the houses which generally surround the bargain house. Now how could you tell a bargain price if you didn't know the regular or normal price?

In short, the learning of housing prices in your area of interest is to help you determine what to buy the house for and what to sell (if you were going to sell) the house for. A great deal of profit in real estate is directly related to the owner's ability to predict these two figures accurately. The problem comes when a house appears to be a bargain when in fact it is not. For example, suppose you found a house priced at 20K in an area where most houses were going for 30K. Would that be the kind of house to buy? The answer is not easy. If the house needed only a paint job and grass seed and a few flower bushes, the answer would probably be yes. These repairs could take only one month or less and maybe cost 1.5K in expenses leaving you with a profit of 8.5K for a month's work if the house was up to the neighborhood standards of 30K. Obviously, if that house needed a new heating system and storm windows to be up with the neighborhood standard, that house would not be a deal. But if it needed a heating system, storm windows, painting and landscaping but you could buy the place for 4K at a city auction, then you *might* want to give the matter some of your closer attention.

The whole purpose of knowing the housing values is to figure out ahead of time how much equity or value you want to have in your completed project.

If you say, "I will not do any project unless I can do it in six months time (working evenings, weekends, holidays, etc.) and "make" 12 thousand dollars," then you have given yourself guidelines for the purchase and improvement of your property. It means in a neighborhood where the houses cost an average of 36K, you will not look at any house where the houses cost and the cost of labor and improvement materials (such as lumber, pipes, carpet, windows, electrical wiring, etc.) will add up to a figure higher than 24K. If it totals 24K but could sell for 36K, then you have 12 thousand dollars of a value sitting in the property as *equity*. Most of this equity you could receive in your hand if you sold the property under normal conditions. Your goal in this phase is to not sell the houses but build up a net value in the number of equities that you build up in various properties.

2. WHOLESALE BUYING

Wholesale buying simply means buying an item below the market value or below the price a reasonable person would expect that property to sell for. How does that happen? Well, a house is a person's biggest and most expensive investment in most instances. When times get hard, people sometimes find that they just can't make the payments anymore and they lose their house or they sell their houses to get whatever money they can get for it *out* before they lose it. Either situation is an unnatural selling situation and causes the price to be less than it normally would be under normal situations. Listed below are situations where you might expect to pay below market value prices for properties.

   a) Sheriff's sale. A sale of this kind takes place when a person has lost his house and the bank wants their money. The bank has the sheriff to sell the house at a public auction at whatever price the public is willing to pay for the house. Naturally, the house is in need of repairs and does not get purchased for anything close to its true value. A 25K type of house may sell for 10K or less.

   b) Fire Damage. When a house has a fire, the owner may decide to do something else with his money besides repairing his or her house. That means a house may be available cheap.

   c) Estate Sale. If a person dies leaving a house that no remaining family member wants, there is usually an estate sale. The heirs want either top money or quick money. If they want top money, they improve the house and seek the top price. If they are in a hurry, they may sell the house "as it is" and take whatever they can get. It is in the "as is" type of situations that good deals can be made.

   d) City Auctions. Sometimes a city will get ownership of a house before the bank gets a chance to sell it. The city is losing tax money that somebody could be paying them as long as that house

is kept out of private hands. Cities auction houses cheaply because they want to see people in houses and paying real estate
taxes into the city treasury.

e) Federal Housing Administration Bids (F.H.A. Auction). The federal housing programs enable millions of people to own homes
that they could not have otherwise purchased. But the F.H.A.
often gets stuck with some of the houses that they have insured.
They offer these homes to the public in a variety of ways including
a process similar to an auction. Sometimes a bargain can be picked
up through this means.

There are many ways to get a house at below the going rate. The
literature listed at the end of this book will add to the methods described
above.

3.   BUYING HOMES WITH NO MONEY DOWN

Any purchase of property requires a pretty good sum of money out
of the buyer's pocket in most cases. This is especially true in bargain
purchases because banks will not lend mortgage money on houses in need
of extensive repairs. But the house has to need extensive repairs in order
to be bought at a rock bottom price in the first place. So where does the
money come from? Out of the buyer's pocket, that's where, unless they
have some private source of funding. The best situation, however, is to
buy the house with *no money down at all*. To own a house with no money
down is to put yourself in a situation where a higher percentage of the
dollars returned to you represent a profit. This might sound like a rather
difficult thing to do, and though it doesn't come up everyday, it can happen
more often than you think.

What kind of situations are those where you can get a house for
nothing down? There are situations where the buyer for some reason
doesn't need the money equity of his or her house in their hand right away
because there are other situations which have more immediate importance.
They do need some strong form of assurance that they will get their
money from the new buyer and that there will be no hassle in getting
such money.

One common method of the no money down type of purchase is the
rent with option to buy technique. If you are not familiar with real estate
principles, please read the next paragraph slowly and carefully so you
can digest all the things that are happening at the same time.

Clara Jones is 80 years old, sickly and living alone in a suburb of a
small northern city. When two violent crimes happen near her home, she
decides to return to the South to live with her children. Clara has lived
in her house for 30 years and it has very old-fashion kitchen and bath

fixtures. It is not fit to put on the general housing market. Through your team members you find out about the house and suggest a rent with option to buy agreement. This means that a contract is drawn up with all the information necessary to actually purchase the house including price, credit history, etc. But this contract is not signed. You will agree to rent the house; and if you decide after a year of living in the house as a tenant that you wish to buy the house, you will then sign the agreement and the sale will take place. Let us say that the rent is $250 per month. In the sale agreement it is stated that one-half of the rent money will be to your credit as a downpayment at the end of one year. That means that if you decide after a year to buy the house, you will already be given a credit of $1,500 (or half your rent money) as a downpayment. Mrs. Jones goes South and you now take over the house. The house is in a good neighborhood even though a couple of crimes did take place in the area recently. The 35K price for the house is a steal of a deal even with the old-fashioned fixtures and other repair work because the other houses around this one go for 50K to 60K.

Now since you have your own house, you need to find a tenant for this house. You find a college couple who are willing to pay $200 a month but also agree to help you with some of the painting and other repair work. They find this kind of work fun and they have plenty of spare time.

Because you have good credit, you are able to borrow $5,000 in a day. After making a list of repairs to be done, you go out and buy modern kitchen and bathroom sets on sale. On weekends and some evenings you come by the house and do the repair work. Your college couple get enthused as they see their living space improving, and they paint and fix up more than you expected. Meanwhile, you have to go into "your pocket" for fifty dollars every month to add to the rent that you send to Clara down South.

At the end of one year you have all of the following situations going in your favor:

    a) Property values for the whole area have gone up 10% meaning most houses are valued from 55K to 71.5K.

    b) You have already agreed to buy this house for 35K by the agreement drawn up the year before.

    c) You have spent 5K out of your credit line for repairs as well as $600 in additional rent payments. Most importantly, however, is the labor and time you and your tenants have given over the year to improve the place.

    d) When you agree to buy the house you go to a bank for a mortgage. The bank sends a lending officer out to the house and he looks

the house and the neighborhood over and says, "We think the
house is worth 60K and we will lend you 80% of that or 48K."
- e) You owe Clara Jones 33.5K (remember the credit of 1.5K for
rent payments).
- f) Follow the mathematics of this situation: The bank lends you
48K and you pay Clara 33.5K leaving you with 14.5K. From this
14.5K you pay back the bank which lent you the money to repair
the place and make rent payments. (5K + $600 + interest = 6K)
You have over 8 thousand dollars in your pocket which is a very
good return for the labor and time you put into fixing up the house.
But you also have 12K of value built into the house; 12K of
equity that you can add to your net assets.
- g) The college couple leaves and a new couple is found who are
willing and able to pay a higher rent. The rent pays the mortgage
note each month.
- h) The next year values increase another 10% and the house is
worth 6K more.

If you study this situation carefully, you will see that not only was
there no downpayment, but the owner walked off with 8K and never,
never pulled a single of his own dollars out of his pocket at any time.

This is how the pros do it and you can be a pro too. If the owner
had not been able to do all the work himself, he or she would have just
borrowed the money for the experts to do some of it and walked away
with less cash. This is the big advantage of learning how to do a lot of the
home improvement work yourself.

4.   DO AS MUCH OF THE REPAIR WORK AS POSSIBLE YOURSELF

This idea is illustrated above. If you cannot do some things yourself,
you do not necessarily have to pay top dollar for someone who can.
There are many unemployed, trade school vocational school and construction apprenticeship program people frustrated and on the streets.
Form a steady team of workers to help you with your projects.

5.   USE BORROWED MONEY FOR REPAIRS

This idea was also shown in the example above. This may be a time
to use your banker teammate. Also, remember all interest paid is tax
deductible. The 8.5K the owner received above is not taxable because it
was part of a mortgage which is *a loan*. The loan is paid back not by you
but by the tenants. The interest on the mortgage and the taxes on the
house are other tax deductions for you (but actually paid by the tenants).

6. Consider Splitting the Living Unit

Suppose Mrs. Clara Jones' house above was a *big* old house. If you could get the town's permission (called a variance), you could split this one-family into a two-family and that really increases the value of a house. This is done very often in the Black community because many families cannot afford the expenses of renting a whole house. Of course, this means two new bathrooms and kitchens, but if you borrow the money and get it paid back by somebody else through rent, what do you care?

7. Sell Only if Necessary

The purpose of this real estate building process is to get enough equity to go in a bank and borrow 50, 75 or 100K to start a business. If racism or other conditions prevent banks from lending you money (but you have a banker as part of your team, remember), you can always sell the properties and get the money in your hands that way.

*   *   *

In this chapter I have tried to do very quickly what I accuse high schools and colleges of not doing, namely to explain some of the fundamental aspects of the real estate world and how they affect us (or could affect us). Some of you may find that I did my job well and many things are a lot clearer now. Others of you may feel that I have put forth so many contradictory, confusing and conflicting ideas that you don't know what I'm trying to say. For that I apologize. One thing, however, I hope is clear and if you leave this chapter understanding just this one idea, then we have made a beginning. That one idea is that real estate is important and we as a people should own some. It would be a shame if an entire race of people entered the twenty-first century having to pay another race of people for the privilege of living on the planet earth. Wouldn't it?

Working Fa-Ya Damn Self—
Ideas on Business

All the information preceding this chapter was designed to bring you *to this chapter*. It is in owning one's own business that enables people to make big money. As you may already know, however, most businesses fail. As many as 80% fail within the first five years. Black businesses, of course, are really risky ventures, and many negative thinkers look at running a Black business as a great way to lose money rather than make it.

This section is designed to point out ways to avoid the kinds of things that kill Black businesses and to show the way to success. I will suggest ideas which are not easily found in other business books.

I'd like to begin by explaining what I mean when I used the word business. A business is:

a) An opportunity to work longer hours and to give more of your love, creativity and talent to a task than what is provided by most job situations;

b) An opportunity to receive a fair return (money and other goodies) for such additional work output in ways that are not tied to "wage guidelines" or other artificial, limiting, subjective or arbitrary decisions by others;

c) An opportunity to build something of lasting value that can be sold or passed on to offspring. A job's benefits are obviously only as long as the job lasts and cannot be passed on to anyone;

d) An opportunity to gain additional tax advantages and build a substantial net worth;

e) An opportunity to have other people help you build your wealth;

f) An opportunity to give some kind of community service;

g) An opportunity to attract other opportunities or financial investors;

h) An opportunity for a degree of independence, "freedom," and a greater sense of security than jobs can usually provide;

i) An opportunity for a significant identity so that your fellow man can know you exist and appreciate and work with you.

Of course not all businesses will have all these characteristics all the time.

156

But such benefits are clearly possible in most business situations. From a purely gut level, the running of a business allows one to freely think about how to make money every single working day in the year. This is not the case with most jobs (except sales). Employers would have you believe that the most important thing you should think about everyday would be how to do your *job* better. Making money would be looked at as some kind of sick, selfish, social disease.

PREPARATION FOR A SERIOUS BUSINESS

Many people seek to make that big leap from being an employee to business owner and do not make the grade. The reasons for business failure would itself take up at least one book, so I will not even try to list the reasons here. What I would like to do is to show the reader what kinds of assets, advantages, and experiences he or she would bring to their own business if they decided to go into business after following the advice in this book.

a) They would have had extensive experience with working business owner hours. The 70 to 80 hour weeks would not scare our entrepreneur because they would have put that kind of effort and time in previous projects. More importantly, perhaps, would be the understanding and attitudes they would have. They would understand why those kinds of hours are necessary and would have the willingness to continue such hours for as long as was absolutely necessary.

b) They would have straightened out their personal finances in such a way as to know how much they needed to take care of basic expenses and budgeted their spending accordingly. In addition, they would have access to a good amount of cash credit for quick responses to opportunities or emergencies.

c) They would have educated themselves on tax shelters, savings, bargain hunting, etc.

d) They would already be homeowners and would probably have a greater sense of stability and confidence as a result of this.

e) They would have developed a team of experts in law, banking, real estate and accounting as well as the skilled trades who would be available to give crucial advice and assistance in important decisions.

f) They would have had some personal experience in selling and would be well aware of their personal likes and dislikes, strengths and weaknesses in sales. The decisions concerning their new business was made with all these factors firmly in mind.

g) As a consequence of all the things listed above, they would have adopted the attitudes and habits that attract success, money and people.

h) As a part of their real estate investment program, they would be familiar with property purchases, leasing, renovating and utility expenses. Thus, they could evaluate potential business sites with an eye on saving money and creative physical improvements at the same time. They would also possess some of the improvement skills and have access to others who work well with them.

i) Finally, they would have assets in the form of real property. They could borrow enough money to go into business *the right way with adequate capital* rather than on a wing and a prayer.

I would think that the person, Black or White, male or female, with this kind of preparation could not help but succeed in their own business. I would also think that their attitude, experience and confidence would dictate that they try a business with the potential to make them wealthy rather than merely one to pay the bills. To many readers, this may seem like a very long, time consuming way to prepare for business. This may seem especially so in a society that pushes ready made, instamatic, fuel injected success. But when you are Black and trying to make it big in business, it is tough and you cannot be too ready. Actually, I have been careful not to quote a time frame for these preparation steps because time is only partially related to what has to be done. Preparation is more a matter of *steps* than *time*. Some people will own enough properties through hustle to borrow business funds within three years or so. Others may take seven or more. Obviously, some businesses take more capital than others and that will naturally have a delaying effect on the starting time. Concentrate on going through the steps and time will not bother you.

BUSINESS THEORIES

The following information is not in any particular order. The information represents various ideas and concepts I have had about business, and especially Black business, in the last couple of years. They are offered here not as some sort of "expert advice" but as ideas to make you think and consider your own experience and ideas relating to your business goals and interests and your community's responses to such businesses.

BLACK BUSINESS—CAPITAL GROWTH OR CAPITAL CONSOLIDATION

In the 1960's, I was a Black Cultural Nationalist with socialistic (or communalistic) values. I believed that Black businesses should be solely owned by Black folks, located in the community, and patronized solely by Black folks. It seemed so correct, so natural in those days of Black consciousness. It's obvious today, however, that we live in a world economy; that should be clear to everyone. Money not only crosses neighborhoods, it crosses continents. The Russians beg for U.S. wheat, the U.S. begs for Arabian oil, and Mao's successor in China wants "a Coke and a smile" for his one billion followers. Closer to home we see that one out of every ten home buyers in Beverly Hills is an Iranian and that the West Germans may end up with New York's World Trade Center. The Arabians almost bought Madison Square Garden, and the French and Japanese are buying farmland in Tennessee and North Carolina. (They think American farmland is more valuable than the American dollar . . . and they are right!) What does all this mean for Black businesses? It means either we join the rest of the world in the world economic system or we will wither away and die.

A Black business must be respected and supported even if it is not in the community and even if it caters to non-Black folks. When was the last time you saw all Chinese people eating in any major Chinese restaurant? Huh? The Chinese restaurant of America is a *capital growth instrument* for the Chinese people. The capital resources (money) of the Chinese people *grow* because it takes money out of the pockets of White folks, Black folks, Hispanic folks and others and puts the money in the pockets of Chinese folks. This means *financial growth* in Chinatown because *new* money is always coming in from the outside. Some of the money stays in Chinatown and some goes right back out.

Black businesses, as seen in the "Black everything" old days, are *capital consolidation instruments*. All the businesses do is draw the money from one Black source and give it to another Black source. The money is being consolidated or collected into the hands of a few people from the pockets of an already poor people. If no new money (other folks, White folks' money) has a way to get into the Black community, then that community will stay poor and produce a few monied folks who will simply arouse the hatred, envy and distrust of the masses. The masses will then continue to distrust businessmen and the cycle will continue.

In the 1980's, Black folks have got to be a part of the overall national and world economy. For example, look at Charlie Pride. Charlie Pride, for those of you who don't know, is a Black country and western singer who has sold over ten million records in his career. It is not unusual for Charlie Pride to be the only soul brother in a 10,000 seat area filled with folks there to hear him sing. We nationalists may have hated a Charlie Pride type person in the 60's, but the man is an example of what's happening today. He's generated millions of dollars which I know had to have helped *some* Black folks, if no more than his family. But it hasn't cost the Black community a dime because all the money came out of the pockets of the other folks.

One of the best ways to get White folks' money is to go into a franchise business. I believe quite a few Whites couldn't care less if the Baskin-Robbins Ice Cream joint in the shopping mall was Black owned or White as long as it was just as nice, just as clean and had just as many flavors as all the other Baskin-Robbins they had been to. Someday maybe Black folks can come up with some franchises of their own and thereby gain even greater advantages in attracting dollars from outside the community. Booker T. Washington told Black folks in the beginning of this century to "learn something the *World* thinks is important." That advice seems just as relevant now, maybe even more so, than it did seventy odd years ago.

GIVE THE SUCKAS WHAT THEY WANT

Perhaps you are convinced that you do want to go into business for yourself, but you are completely puzzled in trying to choose that business. This is a very common problem and there certainly are many ways to approach the problem. Naturally, the interests of the businessman, his experience and talent and the potential for profit are strong determining factors (not to mention working capital). I have a little theory which I believe has some relevance and you may want to think about it while pondering your dilemma. The theory is simple. Give the suckas what they want. Let me explain to you how I finally was forced into accepting this common business idea.

My last two years of teaching Black studies were very rough on me emotionally. It was becoming very, very obvious that I had been lying to myself for some time and I finally had to face the truth. The truth was that Black students, at least at my school during the mid-seventies, couldn't care less about Black studies. Here I was all hyped up and rapping about Marcus Garvey, DuBois, David Walker and the Klan, and the students were laid back, half stoned and wondering, "Why is this guy getting so excited about these people? Why don't he just cool it?" I also found that the reason that a few students were consistently late or absent from class was because they were watching the soap operas on t.v.! Can you dig that? Black students went to jail to have Black studies on campuses, and these dudes were still into Ivory Snow. Platform shoes, stereo sets, the latest Richard Pryor album—any and every little simple ass thing was more important than the history of the Black struggle. Soon, I began to find myself hating the very students I had come to the campus to love and teach. It was then that I knew it was time for me to go. Actually, I never really hated the students; I hated their sense of priorities, their values and their determination to remain ignorant of the things that *I felt* were important for them to know.

I did not know it at the time, but this was a great part of my business education. I learned what everyone else who tries to work with and please the public (the masses) must eventually learn, and it is very simple. *Give the suckas what they want.*

People want what they want. You may come along as a good guy and try to give people what you think they need, maybe even what they think *they* need, but they will still want what they want. Eventually it will hit you that people really don't deal with their *needs*. They don't buy what they *need* or do what they *need* to do. People deal with their *wants,* period. They buy what they *want* and do what they *want.* They may eventually deal with their needs but only if there is any money, time or energy leftover.

As a businessman, you have to be clear not to confuse yourself in playing one role when you should be playing another. If you play social worker trying to supply a need instead of a businessman supplying want, you will go broke. If after you have made your money and *then* supply a need, you will be a community hero. Let's look at an example.

John owns a bar and makes good money selling liquor. John has a Masters degree in social work but he got laid off in the city budget crisis. Actually, John was tired of working at the Welfare Board anyway. The heavy gossip and sexual politicking really bothered him. Most of all, John hated the heavy harassment he received from some of the welfare clients who never seemed to follow his instructions. Several times they ended up calling him a bunch of S.O.B.'s while he was trying to help them. There was poor pay at the welfare office, and this bugged John too. Everytime he thought he was in line for a raise, the Mayor would holler "job freeze," "pay freeze," etc. John decided to "Give the suckas what they wanted" and they wanted a liquor store. So, he opened a bar and he gives it to them six days a week, sixteen hours a day. The money is heavy. John does not feel good about selling liquor to poor folks, but he feels there is nothing else he can do. What corporation hires social workers?

Two years later, the school board decided that they would have to discontinue basketball in the school system because there was not enough money. John was hurt because he went to school on a basketball scholarship, and he realized many kids would lose out on college if basketball was dropped. John, who has three bars now, calls up the newspaper and tells the sports editor that he would be willing to give 25K to the school system if they could guarantee that they could come up with the rest of the needed funds for at least the next three years. The paper breaks the story on the front page, John is on the nightly news program, the school board brings back basketball, and John is super hero in the community. John's bar business has almost doubled. Now, what happened in this situation?

a) John was frustrated, blocked and unappreciated when as a social worker he was trying to provide *vital* human needs. He was a S.O.B. to the very people he was trying to help. (I'm sure I was a S.O.B. to the very students I was trying to teach.)

b) John "gave the people what they wanted," which was cheap liquor, and he made a lot of money.

c) John was able to provide, almost singlehandedly, a community need (school sports program) and was, at least temporarily, a hero.

John was very glad he was able to help the school system and young people, but he realizes that saving the basketball program wasn't half as important as his helping poor folks with their health, heat and food stamp problems down at the welfare board. Yet, there he was often a S.O.B., couldn't get a raise and was eventually laid off. Now he has a plaque from the Mayor (the same one who blocked his raises), the people love him, and he has nine barmaids collecting money in small baskets each week. He really does not know whether to be happy, sad or ashamed.

The example of John above is only one situation where the successful person becomes so after they decide to deal with wants rather than needs.

Another choice many people have to make is the choice between popular appeal and excellence. In school, you see, we were taught to strive for excellence. It may be very nice to be excellent in what you do as long as you understand that excellence may not always be profitable. Let me ask you a few questions.

Do you know how many excellent and talented jazz musicians have to switch to the boom, boom, boom of rock music in order to consistently eat?

Do you know how many talented poets have to write dumb advertising jingles in order to eat?

Do you know how many fantastic stage and screen actors and actresses have to play some stupid role on those simpleton t.v. game shows to be able to by a decent house in New York or California?

Do you know that your Ph.D. college professor probably makes less money than your trash man and your old junior high school *vice* principal?

Do you know how many fantastic painters have to paint houses and garages to buy food for their family?

Do you know that the average Black lawyer makes less money for each hour worked than the mechanic who services their car?

I could go on forever pointing out the ways where the goodies of society are not always evenly divided and distributed to those persons we were taught to emulate—the smart, the dedicated, the sensitive, the talented, and the skilled. If you go into business to make money, find out what the suckers want and then give it to them. There will be plenty of opportunities to make a social contribution; you don't need to worry about that.

THE $5-$15 ESCAPE

I have strongly suggested that a prosperous businessperson should sell the people what they want. Does that mean that a person should sell narcotics, sex, pills, numbers or hot goods? No, I don't believe a person has to dip into the illegal or socially unacceptable areas to make money in business. He or she can do quite well by selling five to fifteen dollar escape items. What is a five to fifteen dollar escape item? Well, I have this theory that in order to give people what they want and what they will gladly pay for, you have to do two things.

1) You have to offer your product for a price that is between five and fifteen dollars. This is the sum that most people have (or can get) and feel comfortable in blowing in a day or evening. Flea markets are based partially on this idea.

2) The product that you sell must have some escape element connected to it. By escape I mean an item or situation or service that allows the buyer to forget or lose consciousness of their poverty, powerlessness, ignorance, pain, family problems, job problems, or other of life's hassles. People *need to deal* with their problems and try to solve them. But people generally *want to escape* them altogether.

One of the reasons, for example, why people are so concerned with the extensive lighting, sound system, and non-stop music of discos is because the more "atmosphere" and fantasy associated with the place, the closer it comes to being in "another world." What better "escape value" can you have than being in "another world?"

Discos, skating rinks, bars, movies, churches, amusement parks, music concerts, stage shows, sporting events, etc., are *places* of escape. Once the paying customer enters the place, there is a loss of attention to almost any problem short of sharp, physical pain. Beauty parlors, massage parlors, health spas, tennis courts, bowling alleys, and pinball games are *activities* or *services* furnishing a degree of mental and physical escape from the daily routine and pressures. Records, books, liquor, televisions, tape players and fancy decorated vans are *items* that are purchased to seek a form of escape by shutting out the events of the real world and focusing on the atmosphere that the item creates or generates.

If you look over the list above, virtually every item, except for the last three, can be purchased for fifteen dollars or less. Is this a coincidence, or is it something that you should look into when deciding on your business?

DON'T START A BUSINESS

The hardest thing to get money for and the hardest thing to do is to start a business from the ground up. There is tremendous ego satisfaction in seeing one's name up in the window or on your business cards and stationery. But, if your purpose is to make money in bunches and to make it quick, you may be working against yourself by using your time, money and physical and emotional energy to do things that may not lead directly to profit. Starting a business from the ground up requires a lot of things that might not have very much to do with earning profit. Consider some of the alternative ways of getting into business.

1.   BUY AN EXISTING BUSINESS

Businesses are for sale in real estate offices just like houses are, and people sell them for the same reasons that they sell houses. This means if you catch an owner in a "changing neighborhood," or who, due to death, divorce, retirement, sickness or just plain loss of interest, wants to sell their business, you might be able to pick up a good deal. Buying a business from an owner is easier than other types of business deals because the old business owner takes back the mortgage rather than the bank. This means that it should be easier to make a deal if the old owner feels you are capable because it is easier to satisfy a person than a bank. Also, an established business already is making a certain amount of profit so a new owner can be pretty sure what his profits are likely to be. In starting a new business, ideas of profits would be pure guesses. When you invest your time, effort and money in a business, you should have more to go on than guesses.

2.   BUY INTO A FRANCHISE

This nation is going franchise crazy. A franchise is simply an agreement between a new owner and a parent company to set up a branch of that parent company in a local area with certain arrangements made on how the profits are to be split. Fast food restaurants like McDonald's, Burger King, and Gino's are the best known franchise businesses. But today, anything from a Holiday Inn to transmission repair shops can be part of a franchise operation. Although there may not be much room for creativity in these types of situations, you have tremendous benefits. These benefits include training, finance help, national advertising, well-known names, and a good staff to help you over the rough spots. Franchises work according to winning formulas and can attract all kinds of people as customers (national market). There is no guesswork; even the toilet paper is decided for you. But, best of all, you have a staff of pros behind you who *want you* to make a lot of money and will *help you expand* if you want to make even more. Franchises are also much easier to sell when you want to leave business and retire. People are quick to pay a good price for a proven winner.

3.   HELP A BUSINESS EXPAND

Suppose you saw an excellent business that was not for sale but seemed exactly what you wanted to do. You may explore through investigation, discussion and observation the possibility of buying into this operation as a partner. Of course, this would not put you in control immediately of your own business, but it might be a faster way to make the money. You must make up your mind which is the most important (control or money). There are various ways that this can take place, and it could include buying out an unhappy partner, opening a second location and managing that location, or providing the capital that will enable the company to add to the merchandise or the overall operating space. However the deal goes down, you know you have an attorney, accountant, banker and realtor to consult with on your team to help you decide if the deal makes any sense. They are to help insure your financial protection if you do decide to go ahead with the deal.

4.   BACK SOMEONE MORE TALENTED THAN YOU

I have often read where a good business situation is where there is no possibility of competition between the partners because they have completely different skills. It only makes common sense if you think about it. Can you imagine two drummers trying to start a band together? Who would really be keeping the time? If you are talented, your job is to seek out somebody to back you in a business. If you are a plain Joe but you have 100K, your job may be to seek out someone talented to support. Fortunes are made with creativity and the ability to *sell* that creativity. Salesmen are much easier to find than talented, creative people. Please don't get so hung up in doing your own thing and seeing *your* name in lights that you let gold mines walk past you everyday without even so much as introducing yourself. Not all songwriters can sing and all singers can't write songs.

5. Go Full Time With Your Part Time Sales

As part of the preparation for running your own business, it was suggested that early in your development you find at least one thing that you could feel comfortable in selling and sell it "part time." This "part time" sales is a thing which is to replace that second 40 hour a week job. Many of these types of sales situations lead to full time efforts in a very natural progression. It is much easier to gain the use of other part time people in your full time operation if you have traveled down that road yourself.

6. Problems Are a Source of Money

People who solve problems get paid good money. It doesn't matter if they fix your car, your house or your heart; they end up living well. In the Black community, the number one problem is poverty itself. Therefore, if you can help a group overcome a bit of their poverty, you could do pretty well yourself. After you have some confidence in your own selling skills and your products, you should seek to be a community fund raiser. If there are Boy Scout and Girl Scout troops, boys' clubs, day care centers, athletic teams, police athletic leagues, P.T.A., home and school associations, church choirs, or any of another zillion organizations and they need a quick thousand, two thousand or three thousand dollars, you ought to be in a position to help show them how to do that through selling your products. If you have a popular item at an affordable price, give up half the profit if you can get scores of people knocking on doors on your behalf. All you have to then do is collect money and supply the products. Perhaps you can make it an annual or semi-annual thing. If not, perhaps you can interest two or three of the good salespersons to work with you part time on a continuing basis. In any event, when you help people solve problems and make money, you can't help but do the same for yourself. If you sell cars or houses you can obviously forget it. But, if you sell something under 15 dollars, you might do well to consider this idea.

7. The Real Estate Business

Many of you who actually make the decisions and the moves necessary to escape poverty will soon find that real estate is a fascinating field. Up to this point in the book, I have treated real estate investment as merely a means to an end (a base from which to finance a business). It should be made perfectly clear, however, that real estate can easily become the beginning, the end and the total business from which you build your fortune. Most real estate investor businesspersons deal with properties other than the one to four family units largely recommended in this book. Many of the office buildings, shopping centers, commercial buildings, condominiums, and apartment houses that you see are the sole means of support for their investors. The "work" of a successful real estate investor may appeal to you. They get up in the morning, count their checks in the mail and ride to their buildings to chat with their superintendents about the conditions. By the time they finish their chat, it's about noon and time to quit work. If they feel extra energetic, they may visit a few real estate offices or other properties that they may be interested in buying to see what deals there are out there to be made. If they aren't interested in any new buildings, then they go to the golf course, tennis court or health spa, not to *escape* from this world, but to *enjoy it*.

8. SEASONAL BUSINESSES

Suppose the business that truly interests you is more or less a seasonal business. You want a restaurant down at the shore or you want a fleet of oil trucks for the winter. There are many advantages (as well as disadvantages) to having a seasonal business, and the successful operator makes enough money in one half of the year to really live good and comfortable the other half of the year. Six months of freedom is a lot better than two free weeks a year, wouldn't you agree? A young, energetic, and hungry business operator may give serious thought to splitting his or her efforts up in order to maximize their profits, contacts, and experiences in their home town.

Suppose, for instance, that an ice cream store was available for purchase from the owner for a 15K downpayment and the record books showed that you could make 30K a year. You look at the deal and it sounds good, but somehow you believe that 30K is just not enough to live the way you want to live. What do you do? Well, you might look around for another seasonal business to buy for winter time profits. If you could find such a business which also netted you say 30K in profits for the winter's work, you would have a nice income of 60K a year. With that kind of income, you could afford to take off at least four and maybe a total of six weeks a year during those brief periods in the year when both businesses are slow (the fall and the spring). If you ever decided to "half-retire" you could sell one of your businesses either in an all cash deal or by accepting payments over the next few years. Your remaining business would still net you more than what most workers in this country make. Does this all make sense?

9. LET THE MACHINES DO THE SELLING

Let's face it, not all people can deal with the public in face-to-face negotiations. This is to be expected as some people are more outgoing, enthusiastic, and have better communication skills than others. It is important to understand and recognize the fact that you don't have to sell to be in business for yourself. There are plenty of people who do no selling whatsoever and yet collect many, many thousands of dollars from a buying public. How do they do it? They do it by letting their machines do the selling. I think everyone is aware that vending machines take in a lot of money, but if you ever did a day's worth of study, you would be more than a bit surprised. Cigarette machines, for example, collect a couple of *billion* dollars each year in spite of all the no smoking campaigns. There are men who make 50K a year collecting quarters and dimes from newspaper machines, candy, pinball, soda, snack, stamp, and almost any other kind of machines you can name. Not only do vending machine operators have their own magazines, national organizations and conventions, but almost every kind of vending machine operation has its own separate magazines, conventions, trade shows and organizations. It's big business. Let me relate a story to you.

An old high school friend of mine told me about this friend of his who had a Master's in Business Administration from Harvard's Business School. I asked my friend what was his friend doing these days (I was tying my shoe when I asked him the question). My friend said, "He runs this laundromat down on Eighth Street." I must have had an incredible look on my face when I looked up from my shoe, because that combination of Harvard Business School (where the people who run a great part of the world are educated) and laundromat just didn't quite make sense as my ears were picking up the sound waves. My friend caught my confusion and added, "Hey man, the dude is making over 50K a year, he's independent, only 30 years old, and he's got some very deep plans for the future. That's the kind of position a Nigga from Harvard is supposed to be in, if you dig it." "Yea," I said very slowly. "Damn! It sure is a hell of a lot of ways to make money in America, ain't it?"

ADDITIONAL NOTES ON FINANCING A BUSINESS

In the preceding pages I have suggested that the best way for a person to develop a means for borrowing the kinds of sums needed to go into business was to build a solid base of residential property and borrow against the equity or value you have accumulated in those properties. All of this is sound. However, I think it is only fair to point out that borrowing money is a little more complicated than that and thus, I will try to lay out the basic things that people and institutions look for when they lend money.

a) The purpose of the loan. Lenders want to know what the money is going to be used for and how is it going to be spent. Lending money is a judgment decision. Therefore, the only way a lender can apply his or her judgment is to actually see if the purpose to which the money is to be used is a good one. Since it is their money, right up to the time they make it yours, they have a right to refuse lending on what they consider shaky ventures. This has always been a problem for Black folks, since almost all Black ventures by their very definition were considered shaky. The way to deal with this problem is to come up with a good business plan. Even if you convince lenders of the soundness of the plan, you have to sell them on you. The best way to do this is to show extensive experience in the business area, a partner or good employees in the business area, or show how your hired consultants in the business area will be used. Many a lender has turned down a loan with the idea that "it was a beautiful plan but I didn't think the guy could pull it off."

b) Collateral. This has been discussed. Your real estate is your collateral.

c) Who else do you owe. It does a bank no good to see that you have enough collateral for the loan you want if you already owe out great sums of money. By these debts being prior or earlier debts, it would seem that these creditors (people who have lent you money) could go after your property before the bank could get its hands on it. Banks like to have first claim on people's assets, not anything less. The only way they can pretty much be sure of that is to make sure that you don't owe out much money to anybody else before they lend you their money.

d) How are we going to be paid back? In all honesty, a bank really hopes that they never have to deal with anybody's collateral to get their money. Getting money back that way means loss of time, middle men, sales, commissions, advertising, legal fees, etc. In other words, after banks demand collateral, they then want to act like it isn't even important enough to be concerned about. Banks would rather see *on paper* how you intend to pay them back. In order to do that, you have to show how much money you *think* you will make in profits and how much you are going to pay them per month out of those profits. The bank then has to make a judgment decision. If they think your profit ideas are reasonable and you can afford to pay them their payments and feed yourself, then you will get the money most likely. If they think your ideas about the profit are pure dreams and un-realistic, then you will not get the money regardless of what you are selling, your experience or your collateral. It's that simple and that difficult.

BUYING YOUR TIME BACK

I have said in several sections of this book that from my personal point of view, time is more important and valuable than money. You will run out of time before you run out of money. I am well aware that most of what I have written about success and business here suggests long hours and hard work. This is true. In the beginning of your business, unless you are very lucky, clever or talented, you will work longer and harder than the average American worker. But somewhere along that course of growth and progress you should reach a point where you can afford to buy your time back. Let me explain.

When you were a worker, you got paid by the hour or the day or whatever. Someone rented you for a certain period of time and gave you some money in return for what you accomplished in that period of time. When you become a business owner, no one is renting you or pay-ing you for your time. You are being paid as a result of your ability to design and manage your money-making enterprise. The benefit of earning income this way is that there is much less limitation on the amount of money you can earn. The drawback is that for the whole thing to work, you have to put in much more time at the enterprise than you did on your job. Is it worth it? Well, that depends on goo gobs of factors, most of which should be obvious to you by now.

My position, however, is that if you aim for the big time, for the business operations that generate 100K plus, you will be able to rent some management of your own. How will you do this? By building the cost of management into your business goals.

Say, for example, I wanted to make 100K per year selling men's clothes. I would never design and plan a business that would merely make 100K a year in profits. I would plan to develop a business that would make say 150K in profits. That way I would be able to pay capable managers up to 50K a year in salary and benefits. I would have the 100K for myself, but more importantly, I would have my time back. In other words, it would cost me 50K a year to buy my time back. Obviously, no owner is really completely detached from his or her business to the point where they are not even involved with the thing, but I think you see my point. The point is that to really appreciate this life and eventually reward yourself for the hard, long, smart and good work you have done, you've got to make 50-100% more than what you actually think will satisfy your needs. That's the cost of having your cake and being able to eat it too.

SUMMARY

The people who make money in American society are principally those who own an enterprise which is *designed* to make money. The owner spends a lot of time and effort making the enterprise do what it was designed to do.

Black folks have had at least three basic handicaps when trying to do their enterprises. The first handicap was having a weak financial base from which to start a business in the first place. The second handicap was having an enterprise which was not designed in such a way to make any real money. The final handicap assuring a high degree of failure was the general lack of awareness or use of the business building and fortune building practices that always seem to be a part of a successful enterprise. I have tried to use this chapter and this book to address these weak points in the hope that some of us can get some shows on the road.

Information, Motivation
and Programming

The ideas presented in this volume may be exactly what you have been looking for. I may have answered various problems for you, given insight into confusing situations and proven that theories which you have had in your head recently are right on the money. But in the final analysis, this book is merely a series of thoughts on a few printed pages. If there is to be any real change in your financial situation, it is mostly going to be due to whatever actions you take to make those changes a reality.

If you are like most of us, you need to be motivated on a continuing basis as we are all products of our own bad habits, negative thoughts and poor surroundings. Thus, this little section was written to help you do what is necessary to put yourself on the right track and stay there until success is achieved.

The goal of wealth is a goal that will take years to reach. During that period of time you will find that no matter how gung-ho and optimistic you start out, you will hit many periods where you will feel stagnation or regression. You will hit emotional lows where things in your personal life or "the vibes" in your surroundings will seem to tell you that "it's useless," "selfish," or "impossible" to do what you are trying to do. Every successful person in the world, certainly every Black one, has had emotional downs and has had to figure out a way to bounce back. Your quest will be no different.

You will find that you will reach points of confusion where you just don't know what to do. There you will need new information and inspiration. With these you will prepare for a fresh assault against the obstacles in the way of your progress.

Even if you do not suffer any emotional let downs or confusion along the way to your fortune, you will most certainly encounter physical letdowns. There will be periods where you feel lazy, uninspired, and lack the drive and the discipline to plunge ahead and do what you know you should do. I assure you that such things are absolutely natural. As natural as all these momentary setbacks are, however, they must be fought off and fought off continually and successfully. If we submit to our doubts, letdowns and laziness for continuing periods of time, we will be digging our financial grave. Some people need to believe that good things will come to those who sit and wait because that's all they are going to do anyway. The smarter ones know that if they don't do it, it won't get done.

The answers to the battle against letdowns and doubt are information, motivation and programming. You can, you will and you must develop your own sources for these three aids. They are the fuel and energy sources that will keep you running when you would normally stop. I will try to explain the following ideas and tie them all to the main purpose of this chapter.

1) Development of the Vision
2) Understanding Your Own Motivation Patterns
3) Developing the Ability to Program Yourself

1. *DEVELOPMENT OF THE VISION.*

Information, work, motivation and programming mean absolutely nothing if a person hasn't made up their mind what they want to do in life. To many people this is the hardest part of their problem. For Black folks who have only been shown one side of life, it is perfectly natural for this situation to exist. Common as it is, however, it must be overcome. The Fortune Builder must see something in his or her mind before they can determine which foot to put in which direction. It is not necessary to know *exactly* what we'd like to do ten years from now so long as we develop a love or an interest in something that is broad enough in scope that we can learn important skills and information. That information can be applied later to something altogether different should that eventually become necessary. *In other words, start somewhere!* Two of the many things you have to consider when you develop your vision are a) what are the kinds of costs I'm going to have to pay to achieve this vision, and b) what are the final financial payoffs if I do achieve it?

The types of material suggested for reading here are designed to give readers ideas about what can be done and what has been done with people's lives. I would think it highly unusual for you not see any activity, person or situation which does not get you to look at your abilities and potential in a new way. If you have no ideas of what you want to do, bury your head in some of this material until you find an area that consistently strikes your attention and then check it out.

2. *UNDERSTANDING YOUR OWN MOTIVATION PATTERNS.*

The purpose of this Chapter is to assist you in programming yourself for success. But no one knows more about how to motivate you than you do. You must eventually be clear within yourself about what turns you on. How have you been motivated to perform in the past? Why do you think that way worked? Were you motivated by strong support and confidence from close friends and family? Those persons may not be around to cheer you on with "You can do it, you can do it," when you tackle your greatest problems. Were you motivated by people telling you that you *couldn't* do something? Did you respond because you were teased, ridiculed or dared into a challenge that you felt forced to accept? That is not a way to develop yourself and your confidence today, is it? Were you motivated by goals that always came from someone other than yourself? Trying to please Mom, Dad, teachers, friends and employers can make it difficult for full grown men and women to realize that they control their own lives. As weird as it may sound, you may have to begin realizing and practicing the control of your own life.

What is Motivation?

Whatever your patterns of motivation are, you must examine them to see what has made you tick up to now. These patterns may or may not be satisfactory for taking you from poverty to wealth and comfort. Motivation, in the context of this volume, is simply anything which helps you push yourself to your goals faster. This may include ideas which generate energy and excitement or events which help convince you that your decisions and judgment were/are correct. Motivation can be the result of victories over things which use to scare or worry you.

In short, what I am trying to say is that *before* you made the decision to build a fortune, you were probably motivated by things which reflected on you as a person. Your image in the eyes of others was what was important. *After* you make the decision to make a fortune, you must be much less motivated by a concern with how you appear to others and be much more motivated by the *thing* which you have chosen to do; namely, to build a fortune. To be overly concerned with the opinions of others is to put yourself in a position to be turned completely around and confused on an almost daily basis.

3. *DEVELOPING THE ABILITY TO PROGRAM YOURSELF.*

Most of us have a very negative reaction to the idea of being programmed. Many of you probably believe that any sort of programming is limiting or self-defeating and that the goal of mankind should be to reach some sort of "natural state" free from commercial, religious and political influences. I believe that such a pure existence is not possible (certainly not in America) because we are all bombarded with both strong and subtle messages and symbols to influence our habits and our thinking. The only reasonable alternative to this message bombardment, it seems to me, is for a person to at least choose their own programming as much as possible. By making definite decisions about what we will allow to enter our consciousness and influence us, we guarantee our exposure to new and relevant information. By selecting from all the available literature only those sources that reflect new ideas and examples of determination and discipline, we program ourselves for success. In a very real sense, this is exactly what happens in law school or medical school. Students read and study thousands of pages of programming material relating to the world (of law or medicine) that they are about to enter. Law schools and medical schools leave little room or time for other programming to enter the minds of their students. Thus, after 3-4 years you have well programmed doctors and lawyers coming out of school. As a Fortune Builder you will be studying other Fortune Builders and the businesses and avenues through which various fortunes have been made. It is very difficult to do this reading and studying on a consistent basis and not begin to see yourself fitting into this world of high finance and independence. Once you see how you fit into such a world and follow through on your action plan, you, like the law and medical students, will actually *become what you are reading about*. This is self-programming. You will find also that through self-programming the many negative attitudes and situations which are a natural part of poor and Black communities will not be as likely to penetrate you and slow you down. Other individuals will be trying for self-improvement through half-hearted attitudes and actions. In a sense, to be self-programmed is to be almost "high." Instead of the "high" being caused by drugs or alcohol, it is caused by the ideas the Fortune Builder develops to take him or her where they wish to go. Instead of the high leading to a kind of fantasy world in the mind, it leads to real world successes which may *seem* like a fantasy to the doubters and pessimists around you.

All this may sound like extreme measures for one to take, but it must be always kept in mind that the forces which ambitious Black folks must fight are extreme also. Extreme racism in the general society and extreme poverty and negativism in the community are a one-two punch which demands an extremely strong program. You cannot have a strong program without using programming itself.

AIDS FOR INFORMATION, MOTIVATION AND PROGRAMMING

Listed below are various books, magazines and other learning experiences which I believe Fortune Builders will find very valuable in their search for economic security.

FOR SAVING MONEY

1. *The Factory Outlet Shopping Guide* by F.O.S.G. Publications. Contact: Ms Jean D. Bird, P. O. Box 183NZ, Oradell, N.J., 07649.

   If you live on the East Coast you will definitely want to get a copy of this 100 page book which comes out every year. The authors have listed the factory outlet stores for virtually every type of clothing and household item enabling the reader to easily find these out-of-the-way places. Hundreds of dollars can be saved by shopping at these discount stores. Each book covers a particular state from New England to South Carolina.

2. *How To Get 20-90% Off On Everything You Buy* by Jean and Cle Kinney.

   The title of the book fully explains its purpose. It costs about $2 in paperback from Award Books, 235 E. 45th Street, New York, N.Y., 10017.

3. *The Wholesale by Mail Catalogue* by T Print Project, St. Martins Press, 175 Fifth Avenue, New York, N.Y.

   This book lists 350 companies who will sell you top quality goods by mail at a reported discount of 30-90% off regular retail prices. The book is a large paperback for about $5.

FOR GETTING A BETTER JOB

The Professional Job Changing System by Robert Jameson, Performance Dynamics, Inc., Publishing Division, (201) 887-8800, 300 Lanedex Plaza, Parsippany, N.J., 07054.

   There are tons of books on the market on how to get a better job, but I found this book ahead of the rest. Their theory of how to sell yourself not only will work for better job offers but in sales also.

FOR SAVING ON TAXES

Pay Less Tax Legally by Barry R. Steiner, published by The New American Library, $2.95, Signet Books, 1633 Broadway, New York, N.Y., 10019.

   Because almost everybody is searching for a way to pay less taxes, books of this sort are probably the easiest to find. I picked this one because M. Steiner use to be an Internal Revenue agent and therefore brings special insight to the task at hand.

REAL ESTATE INVESTMENT BOOKS

1. *How We Made a Million Dollars Recycling Great Old Houses* by Sam and Mary Weir. $12.95, published by Contemporary Books Inc., 180 N. Michigan Avenue, Chicago, Illinois, 60601.

> I refer to this book as one of my "monster" books because it was absolutely perfect for what I needed. To learn about rehabilitating old pads and gaining equity, you must read this book, period! This is a *must* purchase.

2. *How to Wake Up the Financial Genius Inside You* by Mark O. Haraldson. Paperback, $1.99, Bantom Books Inc., 666 Fifth Avenue, New York, N.Y., 10019.

> If this book sounds familiar to you, it's because its author easily put out the greatest advertising campaign in the history of self-help books. Although the book deals mainly with large apartment building investments (which I have not strongly recommended), it simply has too much information and inspiration to pass up for two bucks.

3. *How You Can Become Financially Independent By Investing in Real Estate* by Albert J. Lowry. $11, Simon and Schuster, 1230 Avenue of the Americas, New York, N.Y., 10020.

> Albert Lowry is an absolute master of real estate investment and this book, a national best seller, is full of creative ideas on investment. This is another must buy "monster" book.

4. *How to Successfully Manage Real Estate in Your Spare Time* by Albert J. Lowry. $15, Capital Printing, 50 Washington Street, Reno, Nevada, 89503.

> This 300 page book tells you everything you ever will want to know about managing property. Anybody can buy property, but the money is made by sound management decisions. Although written for big apartment owners, you will find much of the info can be used by owners of smaller properties.

5. *Real Estate Investment for High Yield and Profit* by Harry Gillig. About $20, published by Institute for Business Planning, Inc., I.B.P. Plaza, Englewood Cliffs, N.J., 07632.

> Do not buy this book until you already know quite a bit about real estate. It is not for the newcomer. Contains many creative ideas about financing, government programs, and even contains model contracts. This institute has quite a few good books. Send for their catalogue if you are ready for the heavy stuff.

6. *Nothing Down* by Robert G. Allen. $11, Simon & Schuster.

> This is another "must-monster" book because it is dedicated to the one single idea that will help make you rich—how to buy a house with very little or no money down.

FOR BUSINESS DEVELOPMENT

1. *Up Your Own Organization* by Don Dible. $15 hardback, about $8 paperback, published by the Entrepreneur Press Mission Station, Drawer 2759T. Santa Clara, Calif., 95051.

> If you buy one and only one book in all of America on starting a business, buy this book right here. Mr. Dible is M.I.T. and Stanford trained, but his down-to-earth simple style can be understood by folks who only graduated high school. One chapter explains *40* places you could look to find money for your enterprise.

2. *How to Turn Your Idea Into a Million Dollars* by Don Kroche and Roger Hankanen, published by Doubleday & Company, 245 Park Avenue, New York, N.Y., 10017. $2.50 in paperback.

> This book shows you how to analyze your idea and how to protect it, manufacture, package, ship and sell it. It has the kind of information they don't talk about much in college business courses.

3. *Money, Ego, Power* by Martin and Diane L. Ackerman. Playboy Press, Chicago, Illinois, or write Ventura Associates, 40 E. 49th Street, New York, N.Y., 10017. $1.95 paperback.

> This book was written by the former editor of the *Saturday Evening Post*. His purpose is to explain to the public exactly what a wheeler-dealer is and gives many examples of multi-millionaires who have made and lost large sums of money. Obviously, none of these characters are Black, but I think this book is important to read so that you can see just how the people in power operate.

FOR INSIGHT INTO SALES

1. *I Can Sell You Anything* by Carl P. Wrighter, Ballantine Books, paperback $1.95.

> The author explains how advertisers push, pull and persuade the average consumer to spend his or her money on the ocean of products available on the market today. As a consumer you will learn how to better protect your limited funds. As a salesperson, however, you will discover what gets people to buy and that will help you, right?

2. *How to Sell Anything to Anybody* by Joe Girard, Warner Books, 75 Rockefeller Plaza, New York, N.Y., 10019. Paperback $2.25.

> The author is listed in the Guinness Book of World Records as the world's greatest salesman, and he has been listed as that every year for the last twelve years. His story of his rise to the top from the streets of Detroit make an interesting story, and some of the principles are just as valid for Black folks as they are for the others.

3. *How to Sell Yourself* by Joe Girard. $11 hardcover, published by Simon & Schuster.

> The same author expounds a bit on the problems and efforts of folks who have it tough in sales including the young, the ethnics, minorities, the elderly and women. Encouraging advice on positive attitude development, use of time and something called "the power of a promise."

4. *The Possible Dream* and *The Winners Circle,* both by Charles Paul Conn, published by Fleming H. Devell Company, Old Tappon, New Jersey, Paperback $3, hardback $10.

> These books do not teach you how to sell but are rather the stories of people who have been successful in sales. In this case the Amway Corporation is the direct selling company involved. Although only one Black person is included in the two books, the books are important because they detail how people's lives can change by simply learning how to sell. Very inspiring in many ways.

FOR GENERAL READING

1. *The Success Trip* by Ross Firestone, Playboy Press, 919 N. Michigan Avenue, Chicago, Illinois, 60611. Paperback $3.

> This book asks about two dozen successful people (4 Blacks) how they made it and how they feel about their success trips. Very good insight can be obtained on topics such as risk, luck, failure, security and challenge. You read the statements of the stars.

2. *Winning Through Intimidation* by Robert J. Ringer, published by Fawcett Crest Books, Greenwich, Connecticut. Paperback $2.

> Probably the most enjoyable reading I have ever experienced was with this nationwide best seller right here. Ringer calls a spade a spade and makes point after point on how it is in the wheeling and dealing world of the Fortune Builder.

3. *The Screwing of the Average Man* by David Hapgood, Bantam Books. Paperback $2.

> Already over a half dozen years old, but it's a classic that is very valuable reading. The author shows the public how he or she is being ripped off by the stock market, pensions, the auto industry and the federal government.

4. *How to Beat the Salary Trap* by Richard K. Rifenbard, published by Avon Books, The Hearst Corporation, 959 Eighth Avenue, New York, N.Y., 10019. Paperback $2.50.

> This volume gives many details of how the author became a million-aire while never leaving his job as a buyer and manager at a department store. Although it contains many good points, I personally think the writer is too conservative and overemphasizes the role of money in the bank and stock market investing.

MAGAZINES

1. *Black Enterprise,* 295 Madison Avenue, New York, N.Y., 10017, (212) 889-8220.

> The most relevant regular publication for Black folks seeking to improve their economic situation. Many articles on the heavy issues that face the Black businessperson and the community at large. Many success stories and an excellent source to gain contacts with the people who are doing what you want to do.

2. *Money Magazine,* Time-Life Corp., New York, N.Y. $1.75 per issue at newstand.

> One of the two most important regular publications for the Black person looking to make money. This magazine is a constantly run-ning faucet of information of who is doing what to build fortunes. Success stories, specials on tax, real estate, bargain hunting, stock and other developments are regular features. At the end of the periodical are many ads where the aspiring businessperson can look over the newest franchise type operations that are available.

3. *The American Salesman* published by the National Research Bureau, 104 S. Michigan Avenue, Chicago, Illinois, (312) 641-2655.

> A how to sell mgazine which gives salespersons a constantly running stream of ideas. One recent article was called "Using Your Eyes in Selling." Now that's getting down if you can get to it.

4. *Changing Times* (Kiplinger-Washington editors). $1.25 per issue, Editors Park, Maryland, 20782.

A family type of magazine dedicated to stretching the family budget dollar. Special reports on things like fuel saving ideas, food shopping hints, real estate trends, tax tips and all other basic cost cutting measures.

5. *Saleman's Opportunity,* 6N Michigan Avenue, Chicago, Illinois. $1.25 per issue.

A what's-going-on-in-the-world-of-the-direct-salesperson's-life type of publication. A top source for finding out what the hottest gimmicks are (before it's too late to cash in on them) and what profits can be generated. Also addresses the common problems of salespersons and includes many motivational articles.

6. *Specialty Salesman and Business Opportunities.*

Almost exactly like the magazine immediately above.

7. *Popular Science.* $1.25 at newsstand.

An idea magazine where you are allowed to see what some very interesting people are doing with machines, problems and new businesses.

8. *Inc.,* $2 at newsstand.

The magazine for the owner-officer of the small but substantial company of a half million dollars or more. Deals with the problems of growth and the many gray areas that million dollar corporations find themselves in.

9. The Big Company Magazines: *Business Week, Forbes, Fortune, Financial World.*

These magazines address themselves to the presidents and top officers of large corporations on the international issues (oil embargo, the European common market, world gold supply, etc.) of the day. Although you could pick up some interesting ideas by reading these magazines, the greater possibility is that the information is too broad to be of any use to you in your immediate goals.

SPECIAL EVENTS

1. Trade Shows

Almost every area of American business activity holds a trade show sometime during the course of the year. The occasion is usually one where all the companies of that particular industry show their products in temporary booths set up in an arena of some kind. For the Fortune Builder seeking to get more info on a particular area of business, the trade show is the time and place to catch everyone at the same time. In one day you can walk away with more written material than you could collect in a year of hit and miss collecting.

2. Start Your Own Business Convention

You walk into a large hotel room or arena and the sight will look like a flea market or a trade show. The difference is that rather than selling personal items, the salespersons are selling whole businesses. That's right! Each sales rep has a fifteen minute rap telling you how much money you can make if you take some free time and honest effort and apply it to their business opportunity. Most require an investment of from two thousand to twenty-five thousand dollars. Going to this business supermarket always gives the active Fortune Builder ideas and insight about how things are packaged and sold and how money is ultimately made. If you ever get a chance to go to one, go! It will be the best three dollars you spend that month. You will carry out a ton of mostly free material, and you'll soon figure out how American business can take all kinds of twists, turns and shapes and still come out green.

3. The International Entrepreneurs Association

Probably the most important single organization for the new Black Fortune Builder to check out. This group does research on "hot new businesses" and prepares a complete handbook on how to prepare for, finance and succeed in that business. The most important single question that Black folks should ask themselves is, "Will this business work in *my* area?" which is likely to include a high percentage of minority clientele. To reach this group, write to:

I.E.A.
2311 Pontius Avenue
Los Angeles, CA 90064

Ask for their free catalog on start-up manuals.

A FINAL MOTIVATIONAL NOTE

I don't know how many Black folks actually intend to practice the wealth generating ideas touched on in this book. Probably very few in all honesty will really get their thing together and do something about their poverty and powerlessness. For Black folks as a whole, that is bad news. But for those few individuals who do make moves to improve their financial situation, that should be great news. Why? Because with all the advantages that White folks have made for themselves, there is one problem that they have and will always have that we Black folks will not have for some time. That problem is competition. You see, so many White folks understand opportunity, work and the wealth-building principles that millions of them try to be successful. The competition is mind blowing and is the reason why their corporate world, their Hollywood world and their investment world is as cut throat as it is. They are forced to do something with their own large numbers.

The Black situation is different (except in the N.F.L., the N.B.A. and the Baseball leagues). So few Black folks understand what to do and so few *want* to understand what to do and so few believe that anything will work that in the end, my friend, you have very little competition.

Take this book, for instance. For over three hundred years it has been needed, but nobody wrote it. Now I wrote it. I have no competition. Over two hundred million people in America and over twenty-five million of them Black, and I don't have a single competitor for a book like this. It's amazing, profitable and sad all at the same time.

If you ever wonder if as a Black person all the work and hassle is worth it, remember one thing. There will be few other Black folks with the faith, the guts and the determination to carry the mission through to its completion. That's sad but that's the way it is. When you get anywhere near to where you want to go, you will find you have little or no competition in your way for the rest of the line. And then, my friend, you will learn what gravy really tastes like.

Love,
Subira

You have now completed reading Black Folks Guide to Making Big Money in America. I hope you have found it to be informative, refreshing and inspiring. I would like to hear from you and establish some type of network for future communication. PLEASE FILL OUT THE FORM on page 184.

Dear Mr. Subira,

I like where you are coming from and agree with at least half of what you say. (Please check one or more boxes.)

☐ Add my name to your mailing list. I'd like the chance to examine any opportunity you wish to share with your readers. I am under no obligation to buy or sell anything.

☐ I'd like to order additional copies of this book. Enclosed is a check or money order of $12.95 for each copy I am requesting.

☐ I'd like to sell your book from my shop, store, stand or business. Please send me information on how I can be a distributor.

☐ I'd like to order a large quantity of your books to sell in our fund raising efforts for our church, day care center, drug program, boy scouts, athletic team, prison group or other neighborhood program.

NAME

ADDRESS

                 City   State   Zip

PHONE   OCCUPATION

MAJOR BUSINESS INTEREST

Send this information to: Very Serious Business Enterprises
                                P. O. Box 356
                                Newark, New Jersey 07102
                                (609) 641-0776